D1319777

TABLETS

OF STONE

& THE HISTORY

OF REDEMPTION

Also by

John G. Reisinger

Abraham's Four Seeds
The Believer's Sabbath
Chosen In Eternity
Christ, Lord and Lawgiver Over the Church
Grace
Limited Atonement
The New Birth
Our Sovereign God
Perseverance of the Saints
The Sovereignty of God and Prayer
The Sovereignty of God in Providence
Total Depravity
What is the Christian Faith?

TABLETS OF STONE

& THE HISTORY OF REDEMPTION

JOHN G. REISINGER

5317 Wye Creek Drive, Frederick, MD 21703-6938

phone: 301-473-8781 or 800-376-4146   fax: 301-473-5128
email: info@newcovenantmedia.com Website: www.newcovenantmedia.com

TABLETS OF STONE
and the
HISTORY OF REDEMPTION

Copyright © 2004 by John G. Reisinger

ISBN: 1-928965-14-8

Requests for information should be addressed to:
New Covenant Media
5317 Wye Creek Drive
Frederick, Maryland 21703-6938

Scripture quotations marked (NIV) are taken from the HOLY BIBLE, NEW INTERNATIONAL VERSION® Copyright © 1973, 1978, 1984, by International Bible Society. Used by permission. All rights reserved.

Scripture quotations marked "NKJV" are taken from the New King James Version. Copyright © 1982 by Thomas Nelson, Inc. Used by Permission. All rights reserved.

All rights reserved. No part of this publication may be reproduced, stored in a retrieval system, or transmitted in any form or by any means—electronic, mechanical, photocopy, recording, or any other—except for brief quotations in printed reviews, without the prior permission of the publisher.

It has been said that a person is blessed
if he finds one true friend in his lifetime.
God has been pleased to give me more than one.

Jacob and Carol Moseley
are dear friends and
faithful fellow-laborers in the
Gospel of God's sovereign grace.
Their personal help and continued encouragement
are in a very large measure responsible for many
of the accomplishments of
New Covenant media and Sound of Grace.

Table of Contents

Author's Preface

I am grateful for the response that the first edition of this book received. This new edition expands the subject matter covered previously and adds some new material. The only major change concerns the identification of the Old Covenant as exactly correlative to the Ten Commandments. I made that assessment in the first edition but subsequently changed my view. Although some individual passages of Scripture state that the Old Covenant was the Ten Commandments, there are also passages that clearly show that the entire Mosaic economy, including the ceremonial feasts, became part of "the Old Covenant." My reasons for changing my view are set forth in chapter two.

I am sure the following question is going to be on the mind of many readers before they get very far in this book: **"If what you are saying is so clearly presented in the Scriptures, why have so many theologians missed it?"** The answer is really quite simple. The Jewish teachers and leaders of Christ's day had the accumulated teaching of all the Old Testament Scriptures that clearly told of a coming Messiah, and they also had the traditional wisdom of those who had preceded them for hundreds of years. Why, then, did they miss the Messiah when he came? How can Catholic scholars study the Bible all their lives, yet miss the fact of justification by faith alone? Why does one group of Christians see the truth of the Doctrines of Grace, yet another sees only man's free will? Why do Presbyterians insist the Bible teaches infant baptism while Baptists are convinced the same Bible teaches a believers-only baptism by immersion? Why do great scientists spend a lifetime investigating evidence that leads to God the Creator, yet find only support for evolution? The explanation in every one of the above cases is the same.

The answer is that each person finds only that for which he looks! When we adopt a comprehensive 'system' of beliefs and are convinced that our system is correct, we automatically close our minds to any enlightenment or change. From that point forward, all of our study will consist of looking for further proof of what we already believe. The Word of God **alone** will no longer be either our sole guide or our final authority. This is one of the dangers of any theological system, especially in a confessional church. I often have seen sincere believers urge discussion of a biblical doctrine with an open Bible, only to have other sincere believers say, "There is nothing to discuss, the creeds have said it all."

I hope the sub-title of this book will not scare any reader. The phrase, 'History of Redemption', means almost the same thing as 'Story of the Bible.' This title indicates that I am going to study the part the Ten Commandments play in God's plan of salvation by grace through faith as that plan unfolds in the Old Testament Scriptures, moves into the New Testament Scriptures, and finally reaches into the life of the church today. The material will be of special interest to those concerned about the biblical relationship between law and grace. I hope to give clear biblical answers that will help God's people to obey the command, *Be ye holy, for I am holy* (1 Pet. 1:15, 16). If this book helps any of God's people to better understand his Word and thereby love and serve our Lord Jesus Christ more fervently, my efforts shall be well rewarded.

I have deliberately avoided the use of theological terms not found in the Bible. This book is neither a theological treatise nor a biblical-theological study. Such studies take up where this will leave off. As we begin to study any scriptural subject, our concern should always be with the Word of God itself. We must first understand what the prophets and apostles actually *said* before we start discussing what they *meant*. It amazes me when I see how far theological writers have often removed themselves in their writings from the actual words the Holy Spirit himself inspired. In this book, I will start with what the Scriptures themselves say before I examine how those various verses fit into a particular system of theology.

Theological terms are helpful as long as they express biblical truth. I maintain that the terms we use must first be established with clear truth drawn from specific texts of Scripture.[1] We should *start* any biblical study by using biblical terms because our understanding should grow out of a study of the Bible itself. We should always start by carefully defining key terms with clear biblical facts and texts of Scripture. The 'good and necessary consequences deduced' from a clear *Bible text* and the 'good and necessary consequences deduced' from a *theological system* are often two entirely different things. I will start this study with the words used by the Holy Spirit himself—asking what the Lord says in his own Word—before I inquire as to what the creeds and the fathers state.

---

[1] See Appendix A, "Hermeneutics and the Trinity," page 137.

Chapter One

The Necessity of Using Biblical Terminology

Before we can ever expect to understand what the Bible *means,* we must know exactly what it *says.* In this present study, it is essential that we understand what the Word of God itself says about the Ten Commandments. We should always begin the study of any biblical doctrine with a clear understanding of the terminology used by the Holy Spirit. Initially, we will look up the meaning of the words 'Ten Commandments' in all the texts of Scripture where those words are used. We will then survey the words that are used as synonyms for the Ten Commandments. This will give us a clear biblical picture of how God wants us to think of the words that he wrote on stone tables at Mount Sinai.

Where do the words the "Ten Commandments" first appear in the Bible?

These words first occur in Exodus 34:28, when the Ten Commandments were written on tablets of stone and given to the nation of Israel as the basic terms of a covenant. Here is the verse and context:

> And the LORD said unto Moses, Write thou **these words:** for after the **tenor of these words** I have made a **covenant** with thee and **with Israel.** And he was there with the LORD forty days and forty nights; he did neither eat bread, nor drink water. And he wrote upon the tables the **words of the covenant, the ten commandments.** (Exod. 34:27, 28)

Some Bible commentators make much of what they call 'the law of first mention.' This principle states that the first mention of anything in Scripture provides the key to understanding the biblical meaning of that particular item or subject. We question how far we can push this rule; however, it is true that the law of first mention is often useful. As we proceed with this study, the significance of Sinai as the setting of the first scriptural occurrence of the words 'Ten Commandments' will be made clear. For now, we can say that the initial introduction of the words 'Ten Commandments' in the Word of God is very instructive. The following facts are presented:

1. The Ten Commandments were written on tablets of stone by God himself.

2. This event occurred at Mount Sinai when God entered into a special and unique covenant relationship with the nation of Israel.

3. The Ten Commandments were specifically 'a covenant document' and were called the 'words of the covenant' when they were written on the tablets at Mount Sinai. *...after the* **tenor of these words** *I have made a* **covenant** *...he wrote upon the tables the* **words of the covenant, the ten commandments.**

4. The Ten Commandments, as a covenant document, were given only to the nation of Israel. *...after the* **tenor of these words** *I have made a* **covenant** *with thee and* **with Israel.**

These four facts should always be associated in our minds with the 'Ten Commandments' when those words, or their synonyms, are used in the Bible. In this text (Exod. 34:27, 28), the term 'the Ten Commandments' is equivalent to the phrase 'covenant' and the similar phrase 'words of the covenant.' Our first introduction to the expression 'the Ten Commandments' in the Bible is "...after the tenor of **these words** I have made a **covenant** with thee and **with Israel...**and he wrote on the **tables** the **words of the covenant,** the **ten commandments."** Neither the Old Testament Scriptures nor the New Testament Scriptures will ever change what this text states about the Ten Commandments. The nature, purpose, and function of the Ten Commandments will always be consistent with this first mention of them in the Bible. They are never called or treated as 'the unchanging moral law of God' either here in the Exodus passage that introduces them or anywhere else in Scripture. To call the Ten Commandments the 'moral law of God' is to use a purely theological term[2] that is without any textual support from either this introductory passage or any other passage in Scripture. We will say more about this later.[3]

It is essential that we firmly grasp and hold on to these biblical facts as set forth in the verses that first introduce us to the phrase 'the Ten Commandments' and its synonyms. We should tattoo on our brains the concept that 'Israel,' 'the Ten Commandments,' 'Mount Sinai,' 'the tables of stone,' and 'the words of the covenant,' are expressions that always go together in the Word of God. Any discussion of the Ten Commandments that in any way separates that phrase from the 'words of the covenant' written on the tables of stone and given to Israel at Sinai does not follow the scriptural pattern for use of those terms. We must read these verses carefully and listen to what they say in order to understand correctly the nature, place and function of the Ten Commandments in the history of redemption. If we do not start our study with a correct understanding of the initial use of the term, we can hardly expect to understand later uses of the same term.

How common is the use of the words 'Ten Commandments' in the Bible?

The words 'Ten Commandments' are only used three times in the entire Bible. This usually shocks people. The words are used in Exodus 34:28 (quoted above) and in Deuteronomy 4:13 and 10:4.

> *And he declared unto you **his covenant,** which he commanded you to perform, even **ten commandments;** and he wrote them upon two **tables of stone.** (Deut. 4:13)*

---

[2] The phrase "moral law" comes from the *Westminster Confession of Faith,* Article 19, Section 3, 5. In answer to the question: "Is it right to accept other rules besides the Ten Commandments?" the confession states, "Besides this law [JGR: Ten Commandments], commonly called *moral...*"

[3] See Appendix B on page 141 for a discussion "Is There a 'Moral Law of God'?"

*And he **wrote on the tables,** according to the first writing, the **ten commandments,** which the LORD spake unto you in the mount out of the midst of the fire in the day of the assembly...* (Deut. 10:4)

These two texts repeat the same facts presented in Exodus 34:28. Deuteronomy 4:13 is even more emphatic than Exodus 34:28 concerning the nature of the Ten Commandments. The verse starts with God 'declaring his **covenant**' and then specifically emphasizes, by using the word *even,* that the covenant made with Israel was the *Ten Commandments.* The New Testament Scriptures never once use the words 'the Ten Commandments,' nor do any of the Old Testament prophets use the term in any of their teachings, rebukes, or exhortations. The writers of the Psalms have much to say about 'law' and 'commandments' but not a single one of them, including the author of Psalm 119, ever uses the words 'the Ten Commandments.' There is no biblical evidence for calling the Ten Commandments the moral law of God.

The only references in the entire Bible to the Ten Commandments *as a unit,* or a specific document, are the three verses that are connected with Israel at Mount Sinai when God wrote the Ten Commandments on the tables of stone with his finger and gave them to Israel as the terms of a covenant document. It is essential that the words 'the Ten Commandments' always be thought of as a single unit and as a covenant document. The individual commandments may, or may not, continue in force, as independent and specific commandments, long after the tables of stone end as a covenant document. We will say more about this later. Many theologians tend to ignore this clear and important biblical fact. Little wonder there is so much confusion and so many arguments over the true meaning and biblical significance of the Ten Commandments. In the Scripture, the Ten Commandments are called the terms of a specific covenant: too many theologians ignore that truth and proceed to refer to them, without a shred of textual support, as the moral law. No writer of Scripture ever called the Ten Commandments the moral law. They are only 'commonly called' that by theologians.

What other terms used in the Bible are synonymous and interchangeable with the words 'Ten Commandments'?

There are at least five other words or phrases used in Scripture to refer to the Ten Commandments, or 'words of the covenant.' We will list them singly and give a sample of their occurrences. The first reference for each phrase will usually be its initial appearance in Scripture. It will greatly help us to understand the nature, purpose, and function of the Ten Commandments if we realize that we may substitute any of the following five terms in place of the words 'Ten Commandments.' All of these phrases mean exactly the same thing when used in the Bible. If your view of the Ten Commandments will not allow you to substitute any of the following terms, then you do not have a biblical view of the Ten Commandments.

1. The Tables of Stone: This phrase, used fourteen times, is one of the most common ways in which the Bible refers to the Ten Commandments. This usually surprises people who have never carefully examined how the Holy Spirit refers to the words written with God's finger at Sinai. Let us look at some specific texts of Scripture:

> *And the LORD said unto Moses, Come up to me into the mount, and be there: and I will give thee **tables of stone**, and a law, and commandments which I have written; that thou mayest teach them.* (Exod. 24:12)

Notice that the words "tables of stone" are separated from "and a law, and commandments." All agree that the tables of stone are special and unique. However, the reason for their uniqueness is not their identity as the so-called moral law; the tables of stone are unique because they are the summary covenant document that established Israel's special national covenant status before God.

> *And he declared unto you **his covenant**, which he **commanded you to perform**, even **ten commandments**; and he wrote them upon two **tables of stone**.* (Deut. 4:13)

In this passage, the Ten Commandments are specifically called 'his covenant', which God wrote on the tables of stone. We must take seriously the words the Holy Spirit uses. The Ten Commandments are a *covenant* document given to Israel alone; they are not an unchanging moral code for all people in all ages. When we look at the actual words in the Bible texts, it is impossible not to see that the Ten Commandments were the covenant terms that Israel was 'to perform.' More laws and ceremonies were added to the covenant arrangement as covenant terms, and the entire Mosaic administration became known as the 'Old Covenant.' However, the Ten Commandments were still treated in a very special and unique manner and were still the summary covenant document kept in the ark of the covenant.

> *And the LORD delivered unto me two* **tables of stone** *written with the finger of God; and on them was written according to all the words, which the LORD spake with you in the mount out of the midst of the fire in the day of the assembly.* (Deut. 9:10)

> *There was nothing in the ark save the two* **tables of stone,** *which Moses put there at Horeb,* **when** *the LORD made a* **covenant** *with the children of Israel,* **when** *they came out of the land of Egypt.* (1 Kings 8:9)

Again, the phrase 'tables of stone' is interchangeable with the word 'covenant', and the covenant to which this specifically refers is the covenant made with Israel at Sinai.

> *Forasmuch as ye are manifestly declared to be the epistle of Christ ministered by us, written not with ink, but with the Spirit of the living God; not in* **tables of stone,** *but in fleshy tables of the heart.* (2 Cor. 3:3)

It is strange to hear men argue that the Ten Commandments are the 'unchanging moral law' simply because God wrote them on stone tables. According to this argument, the medium of stone proves unchanging permanence. Paul argues the opposite. He insists that the covenant written in stone was not permanent, but only temporary, exactly because that covenant was written on stone. This very feature proves how inferior the covenant terms written on it were to the New Covenant written in the heart.

There can be no doubt that Paul's use of 'tables of stone' in 2 Corinthians 3:7-9 is a reference to the Ten Commandments.

Again, we note that every reference in the Bible to 'the tables of stone', like its synonym, the Ten Commandments, is connected to Mount Sinai and the covenant given to Israel. This is the uniform meaning that the Holy Spirit gives to the Ten Commandments when he refers to them as a unit, regardless of which particular term is used. The 'Ten Commandments' and the 'tables of stone' are the same thing with the same meaning in the Scripture.

2. The Tables of Testimony: The second term used interchangeably with the 'Ten Commandments' is 'tables of testimony.' This term is used only twice; both times in the book of Exodus. Again, both references are to Sinai when God gave the 'tables of testimony' (Ten Commandments) as a written record of the covenant conditions that would be used as the legal testimony against Israel if they broke the covenant. No preacher or writer in my experience has applied this biblical term to the Ten Commandments. Such an omission is most regrettable. Here are the two textual references:

> *And he gave unto Moses, when he had made an end of communing with him upon mount Sinai, two **tables of testimony,** tables of stone, written with the finger of God.* (Exod. 31:18)

> *When Moses came down from Mount Sinai with the two **tablets of Testimony** in his hand, he was not aware that his face was radiant because he had spoken with the LORD.* (Exod. 34:29 NIV)

The term 'tables of testimony', like the preceding two terms, is always connected with God's transaction with the nation of Israel at Mount Sinai when he entered into a special covenantal relationship with them. The Ten Commandments, the tables of stone, and the tables of testimony are equivalent terms in the Scriptures.

3. The Testimony: The word 'testimony' is used more often than any other word or phrase to describe the Ten Commandments. The first instance occurs when God gives Moses instructions concerning the building of the ark of the covenant to house the testimony, or the Ten Commandments. Later, when the ark is finished, the Ten Commandments are put into it. Notice that the Ten Commandments are called the 'testimony' and the ark of the covenant is called the 'ark of the testimony.' Here are two clear texts:

> *The poles are to remain in the rings of this ark; they are not to be removed.*
>
> *Then put in the ark the* **Testimony***, which I will give you.* (Exod. 25:15-16 NIV)
>
> *He took the* **Testimony** *and placed it in the ark....* (Exod. 40:20 NIV)

It is significant that the word 'testimony' is singular even though there were 'ten' commandments written on the tablets. It confirms that the Ten Commandments are considered as one single document, and that document is the covenant, or testimony, between God and Israel. We could read the above verses and substitute either the word 'covenant' or the words 'Ten Commandments' for the word testimony since they all mean exactly the same thing.

This truth is further confirmed when we discover that the Hebrew word for testimony is sometimes translated 'witness.' The tabernacle is sometimes called the tabernacle of *testimony* and sometimes it is called the tabernacle of *witness.* (See Exod. 38:21, Num.1:50, 53; 10:11; 17:7, 8; 18:2).

It is vital to see the Ten Commandments as the summary terms of the Old Covenant made with Israel. The Ten Words will furnish the witness, or ground of condemnation, when Israel fails to perform the terms of the covenant: the Ten Commandments, written with the finger of God on the tables of the covenant.

4. The Words of the Covenant: The fourth synonym used by the Holy Spirit for the Ten Commandments is the phrase 'the words of the covenant.' These words demonstrate beyond question that the Ten Commandments are the covenant document that established Israel as a nation, or body politic, at Mount Sinai. The Ten Commandments are expressly called the *words of the covenant*. Notice this fact in the following text:

> *And he was there with the LORD forty days and forty nights; he did neither eat bread, nor drink water. And he wrote upon the tables the **words of the covenant, the ten commandments.*** (Exod. 34:28)

It is impossible to read these words and then refuse to equate, in this text, the Ten Commandments with the words, or terms, of the covenant made with Israel at Sinai. The Holy Spirit is quite clear and explicit—"*he wrote upon the tables the **words of the covenant, the ten commandments.***"

> *And he declared unto you **his covenant**, which he **commanded you to perform**, even **ten commandments**; and he wrote **them** upon two **tables of stone.*** (Deut. 4:13)

Again, as in the previous three cases, the text references the 'words of the covenant' back to Mount Sinai when God gave the Ten Commandments to Israel as covenant terms. This fact is inescapable in these texts. They explicitly state that the *words of the covenant* were the *Ten Commandments.* The 'Ten Commandments', the 'tables of stone', the 'tables of testimony', the 'testimony', and the 'words of the covenant' are all the same item in the Scriptures. They are interchangeable terms.

5. The Tables of the Covenant: The fifth phrase that the Bible uses as a synonym for the Ten Commandments is the 'tables of the covenant.' Moses used this phrase at the second giving of the law in Deuteronomy. It is clear that Moses wanted to impress the word 'covenant' on Israel's mind when he reminded them of God's giving the Ten Commandments as the terms of the covenant written on the tables of the covenant. It is not possible to read the following instructions of Moses without seeing that the tables of the covenant are, in this text, the exact same thing as the Ten Commandments:

> *When I was gone up into the mount to receive the tables of stone, even the **tables of the covenant** which the LORD made with you, then I abode in the mount forty days and forty nights, I neither did*

*eat bread nor drink water: And the LORD delivered unto me **two tables of stone** written with the finger of God; and on them was written according to all the words, which the LORD spake with you in the mount out of the midst of the fire in the day of the assembly. And it came to pass at the end of forty days and forty nights, that the LORD gave me the **two tables of stone,** even the **tables of the covenant.** (Deut. 9:9-11)*

Moses, on this occasion, refers to when God, at Sinai, gave the tablets of the covenant upon which he had written the Ten Commandments. The NIV, in one instance, adds the word 'stone' to the phrase 'tablets of the covenant.' This occurs in Hebrews:

*...which had the golden altar of incense and the gold-covered ark of the covenant. This ark contained the gold jar of manna, Aaron's staff that had budded, and the **stone tablets of the covenant.** (Heb. 9:4)*

The ninth chapter of the book of Hebrews contrasts the ministry of Aaron in the earthly tabernacle in the midst of Israel with the ministry of Christ in the true tabernacle in heaven itself. Again, the idea of *covenant* is the recurring theme in this chapter. Verse 4 tells us that the stone tables of the covenant were kept in the ark of the covenant in the Most Holy Place behind the veil. We must remember that not only the ark, but also the *whole tabernacle* was designed in reference to the tables of the covenant. All of the sacrifices and the entire ministry of the priests revolved around the covenant document, the Ten Commandments, in the ark of the covenant. The entire system of Judaism illustrated the truth that there was no approach to God until the terms of the covenant, housed in the ark and shielded by the curtain, had been met:

*The Holy Spirit was showing by this that the way into the Most Holy Place had **not yet been disclosed** as long as the first tabernacle was still standing. This is an illustration for the present time, indicating that the gifts and sacrifices being offered were not able to clear the conscience of the worshiper. (Heb. 9:8, 9 NIV)*

For the law having a shadow of good things to come, and not the very image of the things, can never with those sacrifices which they

*offered year by year continually make the comers thereunto perfect.
For then would they not have ceased to be offered? because that the
worshippers once purged should have had no more conscience of
sins. But in those sacrifices there is a remembrance again made of
sins every year.* (Heb 10:1-3)

The inability of all of the ministries connected with the Old
Covenant to 'cleanse the *conscience*' in these texts is linked to
the closed access to 'the way into the Most Holy Place.' The
writer of Hebrews shows that the 'once for all' sacrifice of Christ
overcame this inability and forever opened the way into the Most
Holy Place. The author contrasts the ineffectiveness of the sacrifice of animals with the highly effective, better sacrifice of
Christ. He tells us, in verse 15, the specific reason for the need of
nothing less than the shed blood of the Son of God himself to establish the New Covenant:

> *For this reason* [to effect what the Old Covenant could not]
> *Christ is the mediator of a new covenant, that those who are called
> may receive the promised eternal* [not just one year] *inheri-
> tance—now that he has died* [under the curse of the covenant in the
> ark] *as a ransom to set them free* [Galatians 4:4-6] *from the sins
> committed under the first covenant.* (Heb. 9:15 NIV)

None of the sins against the Old Covenant were truly atoned
for until the actual death of Christ on Calvary. There was no real
propitiation until the Cross. Every ounce of animal blood shed on
the altar was merely an 'I.O.U.' At the Cross our blessed Lord
picked up every one of those I.O.U.s and paid them in full. The
atoning work of Christ gave him the right to send the gift of the
Holy Spirit. The coming of the Holy Spirit on the day of Pentecost was the heart of the promise in the Old Testament Scriptures
(Acts 2:32-33). However, that promise could not be fulfilled as
long as the tabernacle system was still in force; and the tabernacle system had to stand as long as the covenant terms (Ten Commandments) in the ark of the covenant were in force as the foundation of God's covenantal relationship to Israel. It all stands or
falls together.

As in the other examples, we see again that the same ingredients always go together when the Ten Commandments, or one of their synonyms, is used. The *Ten Commandments,* the *tables of stone,* the *tables of the testimony,* the *testimony,* the *words of the covenant,* and the *stone tables of the covenant* all mean exactly the same thing in the Bible. All six terms are interchangeable. We doubt that anyone can look at the preceding verses and question what has been said. As we will see later, some people may have difficulty applying these facts to their theological system. For instance, if a person says, "I believe the Ten Commandments are the rule of life for a Christian today," that person should realize that he is also saying, "I believe the words or terms of the covenant given to Israel and kept in the ark of the covenant are the Christian's rule of life for today." Both statements mean *exactly the same thing according to the Bible.*

The first time I listed the preceding terms that are synonymous with the words 'the Ten Commandments' on a chalkboard, a man asked, "Why did you not list some of the verses in the Bible that speak of the moral law when referring to the Ten Commandments?" He was quite surprised when I replied, "No such references were listed simply because *there are none!"* The Bible does not even *use* the term 'moral law'[4] let alone *equate such a term with the Ten Commandments.*

I may be jumping ahead a bit, but it might be a good idea to mention the fact that the term 'moral law' is a theological term and is not a biblical term in any sense whatsoever. The term may, or may not, be a correct and useful term if it can be proven to be scripturally correct. However, the term would first have to be established with texts of Scripture that clearly define the doctrine implied or stated in the term. Apart from one instance, I have never seen this attempted with the term 'moral law.'[5] The term is

---

[4] The NIV uses the word one time.

[5] See Tom Wells, "The Meaning and Source of Moral Law," in *New Covenant Theology,* Tom Wells and Fred Zaspel (Frederick, MD: New Covenant Media, 2002), 161-67.

just assumed to be correct. Some laws that we consider ceremonial in nature—circumcision, for example—carried the death penalty for violation. Other laws we consider "moral," such as murder and adultery, were also punished by death. Was it a 'moral' obligation to circumcise a child or was it only a 'ceremonial' duty? Was it a 'moral' or a 'ceremonial' duty to not murder? Is there any inherent difference between murder and circumcision if God gives both laws and both carry the death penalty for disobedience? How can one of these sins be put on the 'moral' list and the other one be put on a 'ceremonial' list? Is there any evidence at all in the Scriptures that the Israelite ever looked at his duty to God in this fashion? I am sure you can see that the concept of 'moral law' creates confusion simply because it is not a biblical concept.

I will discuss the term 'moral law' later. At this point, I am only interested in what the Word of God itself says and not in the non-biblical terms developed by theologians and then used as the essential means necessary to teach a particular system of theology. My question is this: "How does God himself want us to think and speak about the words 'the Ten Commandments'?" The answer is simple if we follow the Holy Spirit's example in the Bible and use the terminology that he has inspired. We will always think *covenant*.

Perhaps it would be good to take some of the cited texts of Scripture that use the five different terms as synonyms when referring to the Ten Commandments and summarize exactly what the Bible itself says about the Ten Commandments. The following statement is composed of condensed Bible texts put together into one definitive statement of the biblical treatment of the tablets of stone:

> God entered into a special and unique covenant relationship with the nation of Israel at Mount Sinai. The basic terms of that covenant are sometimes called the **Ten Commandments;** other times they are called the **book of the covenant.** The Ten Commandments are also sometimes called the **first**

covenant, or Old Covenant, especially when the Old Covenant is contrasted with the **New Covenant** that replaces it. At other times, the Scripture uses the terms First and Old Covenant to refer to the whole Law of Moses.

The **first covenant** was made only with the nation of Israel at Mount Sinai. The actual '**words of the covenant**' are the **Ten Commandments** as they were written on **tables of stone** with the finger of God. This covenant document is also called the **tables of testimony,** or just the **testimony.** The **book of the covenant,** which originally contained the whole of Exodus 20 through 23, was the actual covenant document sprinkled with blood at the covenant-making ceremony in Exodus 24:1-8. There were more laws, including those that regulate all of the Feasts and various Sabbaths, added to the book of the covenant and considered part of the **Old Covenant.** The terms **Ten Commandments, tables of stone, tables of testimony, testimony, words of the covenant,** and **stone tablets of the covenant** are one and the same in the Scriptures. All of these terms mean exactly the same thing and they are all interchangeable with each other.

If this statement causes either confusion in our thinking or problems with our theology, we are not thinking in biblical terms when we consider the Ten Commandments. If the clear biblical facts set forth in the verses of Scripture previously quoted, and just now summarized *in the terminology of Scripture* in the above statement, are new to us, then our thinking in reference to the Ten Commandments has not been biblical! I repeat; we must learn to use *biblical terminology.* We should start our study of any Bible doctrine with a clear understanding of the actual verses of Scripture that discuss that specific subject. I have yet to see a discussion of the Ten Commandments that lists and discusses the biblical references to the Ten Commandments as I have just done.

Most people are amazed that the New Testament Scriptures never once use the words Ten Commandments. It is possible that these people, when they study the subject of the Ten Commandments, have not looked up the actual verses in the Bible where God himself speaks about the Ten Commandments. Perhaps if they had done this, and seriously considered what they had read, some of their conclusions, and surely their terminology, would be radically different.

Summary

The Bible always connects the Ten Commandments with Israel at Mount Sinai. The Ten Commandments were the 'words of the covenant' that were written on the tables of stone and put in the ark of the covenant. The terms the *Ten Commandments,* the *tables of stone,* the *tables of testimony,* the *tables of the covenant,* and the *words of the covenant* all refer to the same thing in the Scriptures. They are interchangeable terms.

We are never told or encouraged to think of 'unchanging moral law' when we read the words 'Ten Commandments' or any of its synonymous terms. We are to think 'covenant document.' We are to think of a specific code of law (the Ten Commandments) that was made the covenant terms of a specific covenant document. We are always to remember that the Ten Commandments were the specific terms, written on stone tablets, of the covenant that established Israel's special relationship with God. The Ten Commandments, Israel, Sinai, and covenant all go together.

The individual duties ordered in the various commandments are a different story. The Ten Commandments, considered as a covenant document, have been replaced by the New Covenant. The individual commandments stand, fall, or are changed according to Christ's treatment of them. Nine of them are clearly repeated, with some changes, under the laws given to the New Covenant people of God in the New Testament Scriptures and therefore are just as binding today as when given at Sinai.

Chapter Two

The Old, or First Covenant and the Ten Commandments

It seems on the surface that Scripture distinguishes between the actual *covenant document* (the tablets of stone) and all of the additional laws that make up the law given at Sinai and in Moab. It is clear from the Old Testament Scriptures cited thus far and passages like Hebrews 9:4, 5 that the 'first, or Old Covenant,' was considered to be the tables of the covenant, or the Ten Commandments. In the first edition of this book, I insisted that we could view the phrases 'Old Covenant' and 'first covenant' as equivalent to the term 'the tables of stone.' In other words, in addition to the five terms listed in chapter 1, we could add 'first covenant' and 'Old Covenant' to the list of synonymous terms. I now believe I was wrong in that conclusion. It is true, as noted, that some texts of Scripture (Exod. 34:28, Deut. 4:13, Heb. 9:4 and others) clearly equate the Old Covenant with the Ten Commandments. If these were the only texts that spoke to the subject, there would be no doubt that 'Old Covenant' and 'Ten Commandments' would be interchangeable terms. However, other Scripture passages indicate that much more than just the tables of stone were considered part of the actual Old Covenant.

Until recently, I would have maintained a total dichotomy between the "*tablets* of the covenant" and the "*book* of the covenant," saying that the "tablets of the covenant," in and of themselves, actually constituted the totality of the 'Old Covenant.'[6] I can no longer do that. It is true that they are clearly viewed as two distinct documents; only the stone tablets were put inside the ark, while the book of the covenant was put 'along side of the ark.' However, it is just as clear that everything contained in the book of the covenant, the Ten Commandments as well as other laws, including those whose sole function was to govern ceremo-

---

[6] I am greatly indebted to Greg Welty for my change in convictions. In a lengthy and detailed email debate, he convinced me that the entire Mosaic economy was considered 'the Old Covenant.'

nies, was considered part of the Old Covenant and possessed equal covenant authority with the tablets of the covenant in the ark. It is clear that the Old Testament prophets viewed the laws that governed ceremonies and civil transactions as part of the Old Covenant demands on Israel. Here are two examples:

> *Thus saith the LORD, the God of Israel; I* **made a covenant** *with your fathers in the day that I brought them forth out of the land of Egypt, out of the house of bondmen,* **saying,** *At the end of seven years let ye go every man his brother an Hebrew, which hath been sold unto thee; and when he hath served thee six years, thou shalt let him go free from thee: but your fathers hearkened not unto me, neither inclined their ear.* (Jer. 34:13-14)

It is clear from this text that the law concerning slavery was a part of the Old Covenant. Likewise, Passover, a ceremonial feast, was a part of the Old Covenant.

> *And the king commanded all the people, saying, Keep the passover unto the LORD your God, as it is written in the book of this covenant.* (2 Kings 23:21)

I think the New Testament Scriptures also teach this fact. I do not believe that 2 Corinthians 3:14 can be referring to the Ten Commandments.

> *But their minds were made dull, for to this day the same veil remains when the old covenant is read. It has not been removed, because only in Christ is it taken away. Even to this day when Moses is read, a veil covers their hearts.* (2 Cor. 3:14-15 NIV)

I would agree with the classical Covenant Theology tenet that the Jews did not understand the true import of the Ten Commandments, but that is not all that Paul is talking about in this text. Although Paul has referred to the tables of stone earlier in this letter to the Corinthians (3:3, 7), the record in Acts 13:15 indicates that what was commonly read to the Jews in the synagogue was the "Law and the Prophets." This is further supported by Paul's practice in Rome, recorded in Acts 28:23: "…From morning till evening he explained and declared to them [the leaders of the Jews] the kingdom of God and tried to convince them about Jesus from the Law of Moses and from the Prophets" (NIV). The result in Acts is strikingly similar to what Paul describes in Corinthians; some refused to believe because they could not see or hear Christ in either the Law or Prophets (Acts 28:24-27). Paul obviously means the Old Testament Scriptures in 2 Corinthians 3:14–15 when he speaks of 'the Old Covenant.' We could substitute the words 'Law and/or Prophets' and it would still mean the same thing. The thing about which the unregenerate Jew was blind was the truth of the Messiah pictured in the ceremonies, sacrifices, and holy days of the Old Covenant. We must remember that it was in these ways the gospel was most clearly preached.

This comprehensive view of the Old Covenant does not mean that any of the laws that were added to the ethical terms written on the stone tables in any way changed those terms. Nor does it mean that the Ten Commandments, viewed as covenant terms, could not furnish sufficient terms to be a covenant in their own right. It simply means that the book of the covenant, as an interpretation and application of the terms written on the stone tablets to specific situations, is a part, along with the tables of the covenant in the box, of that which is called the Old Covenant. Texts like Jeremiah 34:13-20 make it very clear that even what have been called 'civil and ceremonial laws' were considered part of the law of Moses, or the "Old Covenant."

I no longer say that the Ten Commandments/tablets of stone are, one on one, the Old, or first, Covenant. I now say that the Ten Commandments/tables of stone are the summary document of the Old Covenant. This summary sets forth the basic covenant terms of Israel's special relationship to God. These basic covenant terms were expanded to finally include the whole Mosaic law. All of the laws of the theocracy, regardless of their type or nature, became part of the law of Moses, or 'the Old Covenant.' It was the book of the covenant (Exodus 24:8), not the tablets of stone, to which Moses referred when he sprinkled the people with blood, saying, "Behold the blood of the covenant, which the

LORD hath made with you concerning all these words." At that point, the Ten Commandments had been given verbally and were recorded with all the rest of the laws that God spoke to Moses (Exod.20:1-24:4). They were not yet written as a separate document on tables of stone.

It seems clear from passages like 2 Corinthians 3:14 and Hebrews 8:13 that the Old Covenant that was viewed as 'passing away' was far more than just the tables of the covenant, or the Ten Commandments. It was the entire Old Covenant and its administration. It was the whole law of Moses. The 'Old Covenant' that is read with blinded eyes surely has more reference to the great predictions of the Messiah than it does to only the Ten Commandments.

In re-thinking this section, I came to accept the following:

The Ten Commandments were first spoken to Moses and written in the book of the covenant before they were actually written on the tables of stone. A careful reading of Exodus 20-24 will clearly show this fact.

Exodus 19:3-6 records Moses' first trip up the mountain. After reminding Moses of his mercy in redeeming them from Egypt, God instructs Moses to tell Israel that if they will obey his covenant they will be his special people—a kingdom of priests and a holy nation. Moses delivers God's message to Israel (v.7) and they promise to do everything God commands. In verse 8, Moses goes back up the mountain a second time and reports to God the promise of the Israelites. God then tells Moses that he will speak to him and all the people will hear the voice of God and consequently believe that Moses truly represents God (v.9). Moses is told to go down, consecrate the people, and warn them not to come near the mountain or they will perish. Moses goes down, consecrates them, and delivers the warning (v.14). Three days later, God descends to the mountain and Moses again goes up to meet him (vv.16-20). The warning is repeated, and Moses is instructed to return to the foot of the mountain in anticipation of yet another trip up, this time with Aaron (vv.21-24). Moses returns once more to the foot of the mountain, as instructed, and repeats God's warning not to approach the mountain (v.25). It is at this point that God himself speaks (20:1), while Moses and the people are at a distance from the mountain (20:18-19).

Chapter 20 states, "God spoke all these words, saying ..." and then records the Ten Commandments. There is no mention of tables of stone yet. The Ten Commandments were spoken in Israel's hearing before they were written on stone. In verse 19, the people express their fear of God and ask Moses to speak to them. Moses then goes into the darkness surrounding the mountain (v.21) and God gives him more laws. God repeats the warning against idolatry and gives instructions to build an altar (vv.22-26). Exod. 21:2 through the end of chapter 23 records a list of the laws that God then gave to Moses. Moses is instructed to get Aaron and certain others and to then return (24:1-2). When he returns as instructed, Moses repeats to Israel all the laws God has given him, including the Ten Commandments (24:3). Again, the Israelites verbally commit themselves to obey every word God has spoken. Moses then writes down everything God has spoken (v.4)—we assume this includes the Ten Commandments—and calls all of it the book of the covenant (v.7). After building the altar as previously instructed, Moses takes the blood of the animals just sacrificed and sprinkles half of the blood on the altar (v.6). He then reads the book of the covenant and the people again vow to keep everything commanded therein. Moses sprinkles the rest of the blood on the people and says, "Behold the blood of the covenant which the LORD has made with you according to all these words" (v.7, 8).

At this point, God has entered into a formal covenant with Israel. The Ten Commandments are part of that covenant; they were first given verbally and then written in the book of the covenant. After meeting with Aaron and the others, God tells Moses to come back up into the mountain and promises to give him "tables of stone, the law and commandments which I have written" (Exodus 24:12). Moses then returns up the mountain taking Joshua with him and they are there forty days and forty nights. God gives Moses instructions concerning the tabernacle, the priesthood, the offerings, etc. This is chronicled in chapters 25 through 31. In 31:18, we read, "And he gave unto Moses, when he had made an end of communing with him upon Mount Sinai, two tables of testimony, tables of stone, written with the finger of God."

The "tables of stone" were promised in Exodus 24:12, but not actually written until 31:18. We must see the distinction between the *book of the covenant*, which would include all that was recorded in Exodus 20-23, and the *tables of the covenant*, which include only the Ten Commandments. Exodus 34:27, 28 explicitly state that the terms of the covenant God made with Israel were the Ten Commandments. Exodus 24:3-8 states just as explicitly that the book of the covenant, which included but was not limited to the Ten Commandments, was the covenant document. Deuteronomy 31:24-26 is a key passage:

> *And it came to pass, when Moses had made an end of writing the words of this law in a book, until they were finished, That Moses commanded the Levites, which bare the ark of the covenant of the LORD, saying, Take this book of the law, and put it in the side of the ark of the covenant of the LORD your God, that it may be there for a witness against thee.*

We learned from Exodus 25:16-21 that the ark was to house the 'testimony.' Later in Exodus (31:18), this testimony was identified as the "two tables of testimony, tables of stone, written with the finger of God." From those verses, we see that the Ten Commandments were considered the basic covenant document, since the "ark of the covenant of the Lord" was specially built to house those tables. This passage in Deuteronomy shows that the book of the law, although including the Ten Commandments, is a separate document from the tables of stone. It was placed *beside* the ark; the Ten Commandments written on tables of stone were already *in* the ark (Exod.40:20). The reason for placing the book of the covenant along side the ark was to act as a witness to Israel's sin of covenant breaking. Later, the 'book of the law' will be added to by different people, but the Ten Commandments were never changed until our Lord came. The book mentioned in Deuteronomy 31:25 does not appear to be the same book that was sprinkled with blood in Exodus 24:8, yet the later version is still called the book of the covenant.

I should mention several other points of interest. In Nehemiah 8:1, all the people of Israel command Ezra to bring the "book of the law of Moses," and in verse 8 we read, "So they read distinctly from the book, in the Law of God" (NKJV). The book of the law of God and the book of the law of Moses seem to be the same thing. They surely did not take the tablets of the covenant out of the box. Had they done so, they would not have lived to tell about it.

The Scripture speaks of the *book of the Law, the book of the law of Moses,* and *this book.* Moses wrote another "book of the law" in Deuteronomy 31:24-26 and instructed that it be placed "along side" of the ark of the covenant. Joshua either wrote a "book of the law" or added to what Moses had written (Josh. 24:26). Samuel wrote a "book of the law" and "laid it before the Lord" (1 Sam. 10:25). Hilkiah found the "book of the law of Moses" in the temple and Shaphan read from it (2 Kings 22:8-10).

The above 'books of the law' could not be the tables of stone, since no one was allowed to even touch the ark, let alone open it and remove the tablets. Those tables were always treated differently. Originally, they formed the basic covenant document and could be equated with the "Old Covenant." However, the various "books of the law" were also considered as part of "the covenant" made with Israel. The ceremonial system was looked upon as part of the Old Covenant that Israel entered into at Sinai. This is evident from the passage in 2 Kings 23:20-21, when the "book of the law" was discovered during the reign of Josiah, and its reading produced a revival.

And he slew all the priests of the high places that were there upon the altars, and burned men's bones upon them, and returned to Jerusalem.

And the king commanded all the people, saying, Keep the passover unto the LORD your God, as it is written in the book of this covenant.

The law of the Passover was considered part of the "book of the covenant." We know that the law of the Passover was not written on the tables of stone. When Scripture speaks of the teaching of the law of God or the law of Moses, it is doubtful if it ever refers to just the Ten Commandments. The "book of the law" in Galatians 3:10 cannot be equated with the Ten Commandments alone, even though that "book of the law" is given covenantal status with the power to condemn to death for the least infraction. Paul is quoting either Deuteronomy 27:26 or Jeremiah 11:3, which refers back to the Deuteronomy passage. A curse for non-compliance with "the words of this law" comes at the conclusion of a long list of curses for various infractions, some of which are not listed in the Ten Commandments. The list itself is preceded by chapters of instruction, starting in chapter 4 with these words; "Hear now, O Israel, the decrees and laws I am about to teach you..." (NIV). These instructions include the Ten Commandments, but are certainly not limited to them.

The purpose of this chapter has been to show that (1) the Ten Commandments can correctly be called the covenant document, written with the finger of God, that established Israel's special relationship with God. However, (2) it is just as clear that the totality of all the laws given to Israel also became a part of the Old Covenant. The covenant and the covenant administration merge into one entity.

There are several important things for us to remember about the Ten Commandments, or tables of the covenant. First, they always remained in the ark of the covenant in the Most Holy Place. They were unchanged in the slightest detail and untouched by human hands. Two, they were always treated in a most unique way. All agree that the Ten Commandments receive radically different treatment than all the other laws, but not everyone agrees as to why they were treated so differently. Never are the tablets of stone viewed as special and different because they are the so-called moral law. Third, the name of the box that housed the Ten Commandments conveys their significance. That box is unique and holy only because of what was in it. It was holy because it housed the tablets of the covenant that established Israel as a nation and furnished the testimony of her covenant breaking and thus the grounds of her rejection. If the Ten Commandments written on the tables of stone were 'God's unchanging moral law' then the ark would have been called the 'ark of the moral law.'

Summary

The basic covenant document that contained the actual terms of the Old Covenant was the tablets of stone or Ten Commandments. The Ten Commandments can also be looked upon as a summary of the whole covenant relationship between God and Israel. When we think of the Old Covenant, there are two ideas, both of which must be held at the same time. (1) We must see that the Ten Commandments are the basic covenant document that established Israel as a theocratic nation. At the same time, (2) we must see that all of the laws, holy days, priesthood, and sacrifices became part of the 'Old Covenant.' Scripture, in Exodus 24:1-8 and other places, clearly makes this distinction.

Chapter Three

The Problem of 'Two Versions'

This part of our introduction to the Ten Commandments concerns the necessity of knowing exactly what was written on the tables of stone. It is impossible to understand the theological significance of the tables of the covenant if we do not know exactly what is being commanded in the terms of the covenant. We must first know precisely what duty is being commanded before we start discussing its nature and purpose. Nothing but confusion and misunderstanding will result if we are not all talking about the same thing.

What was written on the tablets of stone? Exactly what are the 'Ten Commandments'?

What was the exact content of the Old Covenant document that God wrote with his finger on the tables of the covenant? One would think that such a question is unnecessary, and some may be surprised that we start with something so simple. If we do not start here, and just assume that everyone knows the answer, we will be guilty of contributing to both the ignorance already in existence about the Ten Commandments, as well as the bad theology that ignorance has produced.

It is essential to note that the Bible gives two *different versions* of the Ten Commandments as they were written on the first set of stone tablets. Both Exodus 20 and Deuteronomy 5 refer to the same set of stone tablets. The Exodus account records the occasion at Sinai; in Deuteronomy, Moses recounts the history of that incident to refresh the people's memory. Because of the very real differences in the two accounts, it is not possible that all the words recorded in both Deuteronomy 5 and in Exodus 20 could have been written on the same tables of stone. The following chart compares some of the differences in the two versions of the Ten Commandments as they are found in Exodus, chapter 20 and Deuteronomy, chapter 5. The first through third and the sixth through ninth commandments are almost identical. The greatest differences are in the fourth and fifth. Since our concern at this point is only in the fact that there *are* two different versions of the Ten Commandments, we will only note the differences in the fourth commandment.

A dotted line (........) indicates that something is missing in that particular account, and words in *italics* signify that something has been added that is not in the other account. We only need to glance at the number of dotted lines and words in italics to see that there is a vast difference between the two accounts of the fourth commandment. We find it surprising and somewhat irresponsible that these differences are almost totally ignored by theologians today. Remember, we are discussing the original set of the tables of stone that were written with the finger of God. There cannot be two versions of something that is written on the same stone tablets.

EXODUS 20	DEUTERONOMY 5
8. Remember the sabbath day, to keep it Holy	12. Keep the sabbath day to sanctify it, *as the LORD thy God hath commanded thee.*[7]
9. Six days shalt thou labor, and do all thy work:	13. Six days thou shalt labor, and do all thy work:
10. But the seventh day is the sabbath of the LORD thy God: in it thou shalt not do any work, thou, nor thy son, nor thy daughter, thy manservant, nor thy maidservant,	14. But the seventh day is the sabbath of the LORD thy God: in it thou shalt not do any work, thou, nor thy son, nor thy daughter, nor thy manservant, nor thy maidservant,
.... nor thy cattle, nor thy stranger that is within thy gates:	*nor thine ox, nor thine ass,* nor any of thy cattle, nor thy stranger that is within thy gates; *that thy manservant and thy maidservant may rest as well as thou.*
11. *For in six days the LORD made heaven and earth, the sea, and all that in them is, and rested the seventh day: wherefore the LORD blessed the sabbath day, and hallowed it.*	....
....	15. *And remember that thou wast a servant in the land of Egypt, and that the LORD thy God brought thee out thence through a mighty hand and by a stretched out arm: therefore the LORD thy God commanded thee to keep the sabbath day.*

---

[7] We will discuss, in a later chapter, exactly when God gave this commandment. Some insist it was given to Adam at creation and others say it was first given to Israel at Sinai.

There is a great difference in the fourth commandment as recorded in Exodus 20:8-11 and the same commandment as recorded in Deuteronomy 5:12-15. The entire contents of Exodus
20:11 are missing from Deuteronomy 5, and likewise, all the
words contained in Deuteronomy 5:15 are omitted in Exodus 20.
Moses gave two very different reasons for why the sabbath was
to be kept holy. The first reason, Exodus 20:11, was to follow
God's example in Genesis, and the second, Deuteronomy 5:15,
was to remember the recent deliverance from Egypt. Very few
writers even mention these differences in the two versions of the
Ten Commandments, and most of them make no attempt to deal
with the obvious problems created by the impossibility of having
two different things written on the *same tables of stone.*

A.W. Pink, in his commentary on Exodus, never notices the
problem. Walter Chantry, in *God's Righteous Kingdom,* not only
neglects to mention the fact that there are differences, he also
uses Deuteronomy 5:22 in a manner that greatly compounds the
problem.[8] Chantry insists that when Moses said, "and He added
nothing more" that God explicitly meant that 'nothing can be
added' to the commandments recorded in Deuteronomy 5:1-21.
This would mean that none of the words recorded in Exodus 20
that are omitted in Deuteronomy 5 can be *added to Deuteronomy
5* and then considered to be part of the actual commandment written on stone. Patrick Fairbairn, in *The Revelation of God in Scripture,* is the only writer I have read who seriously attempts to re-
solve the problem.[9] Fairbairn does not mention the further problem created by the words "and he added no more" in Deuteronomy 5:22.

I think it is more than fair to say that any attempt to understand the true meaning and function of the tablets of stone in the
history of redemption that does not begin by clearly establishing

---

[8] Walter Chantry, *God's Righteous Kingdom* (Carlisle, PA: Banner of Truth,
1980), 87, 88.

[9] Patrick Fairbairn, *The Revelation of God in Scripture* (1869; reprint, Winona
Lake, IN: Alpha Publications, 1979), 325-334.

exactly what was written on those tablets is doomed to confusion and contradiction. How is it possible to know the true meaning and significance of commandments when we do not know for sure what a given commandment actually says? Likewise, I feel justified in thinking that a person's understanding of the significance of the Ten Commandments is rather shallow if that person never even noticed that the Bible gives two conflicting versions of those commandments.

What are the implications involved in the fact that there are 'Two Different Versions' of the Ten Commandments in the Bible?

One: The doctrine of the verbal inspiration of the Scripture is involved. We are not talking about two versions of a parable or miracle; we are dealing with very special and unique commandments of great significance that the finger of God wrote in stone. These commandments were the terms of a covenant document; nothing should be more exact and specific than that. It is not possible that God wrote on the tablets of stone everything found in *both* the Exodus 20 version and the Deuteronomy 5 version of the Ten Commandments. Something is obviously wrong, and crucial tenets of the faith are at stake until the problem is resolved. The solution might be a bit easier if two different writers had given the two different versions. However, in this case Moses is the author of both Exodus 20 and Deuteronomy 5.

Patrick Fairbairn uses the basic 'dynamic equivalent' theory to reconcile the two versions. This theory proposes the concept that a writer may use different words or phrases in two separate accounts of the same thing, but the basic meanings of the two are the same. Even if this method is accepted as legitimate, it could not be stretched to reconcile the radical differences in Exodus 20 and Deuteronomy 5. How can the action of God in the deliverance of Israel from Egypt be in any way the dynamic equivalent of the work of God in the creation of the heavens and earth in six days and rest on the seventh day?

The belief that the Ten Commandments, *as given in Exodus 20 and Deuteronomy 5,* are the 'eternal unchanging moral law of God' only adds to the problem. How can we believe that God intended the tablets of stone to be what some preachers, with no biblical proof, insist on calling the unchanging moral law of God, and also believe that God would inspire Moses to give *two different versions* of his 'unchanging moral law'? The fact that we have two versions ought to be enough to alert any serious mind to stop and think. The two different versions of the Ten Commandments must be reconciled to each other before it is possible to know for sure what God actually wrote on the tablets of stone! We have people arguing vehemently about 'unchanging laws' without even knowing what those laws actually say. Listed below are three possible approaches to the problem of the two different versions of the Ten Commandments:

1. The Bible contradicts itself. Every Bible believer will reject this explanation.

2. Moses, in Deuteronomy 5, forgot what God actually wrote on the tablets of stone in Exodus 20 and therefore left out the part about creation. (Fairbairn is weak in his arguments against this point.) Moses also added, in Deuteronomy 5, the part about deliverance from Egypt even though it was not actually part of the original Ten Commandments given in Exodus 20. We must reject this explanation, also. It is merely a rational version of the first approach.

3. It is possible that all that was written on the tablets of stone were the bare commandments. In the case of the fourth commandment, all that would have been written on the tables were the words *Remember the sabbath day to keep it holy.* All of the rest of the words relating to the actual observance of the sabbath, in *both* Exodus 20 and Deuteronomy 5, are commentary added by Moses and not part of the commandment itself as written on the tablets of stone.

Of the three proposed, the last solution is the only position that is consistent with verbal inspiration, even though it might create some problems for some theologians. It would be appropriate for Moses, standing at Mount Sinai, to point Israel back to the God of Creation as grounds for obedience to the newly given covenant sign, or sabbath commandment. As we shall see later, the seventh-day sabbath was the specific sign of the Mosaic covenant that established the nation of Israel as a body politic at Mount Sinai. It would be just as appropriate for Moses to remind Israel, at the second giving of the law in Deuteronomy 5, of God's redemptive rights over Israel because of their recent deliverance by blood and power from Egypt. The two reasons together combine the creation rights and redemptive claims of God over his chosen nation and furnish a double obligation for obedience to the covenant sign and thus the covenant for which the sign stands. This makes for great preaching; we must consider, however, the strong probability that neither of the two different reasons given by Moses for keeping the seventh day holy were part of the actual commandments, or covenant terms, that God wrote on the tablets of stone. Both reasons are commentary added by Moses to enforce the great significance of the covenant sign (sabbath) that had just been given to Israel.

Two: This has an effect on our understanding of the sabbath commandment. It is impossible to use Exodus 20:11 to prove that the seventh-day sabbath was a so-called 'Creation ordinance.' You must add the Creation argument to the version given in Deuteronomy 5 before you can make it part of the actual commandment. However, as Walter Chantry has clearly demonstrated, Deuteronomy 5:22 forbids any such additions:

1. "God spake 'these words'" (Deut. 5:22) refers to the words just spoken in Deuteronomy 5:1-21.

2. There is no mention at all of Creation in Deuteronomy 5, just as there is no mention of deliverance from Egypt in Exodus 20.

3. Moses is emphatic that God 'added no more' to the words just written in Deuteronomy 5:1-21.

The purpose of Chantry, in the section where he quotes Deuteronomy 5:22, is to prove that the seventh-day sabbath is a Creation ordinance. It is surprising that he did not realize that his comments on Deuteronomy 5:22 make it impossible to use Exodus 20:11 as proof that the sabbath began at Creation. In order to make Exodus 20:11 to be a part of the fourth commandment, Chantry must clearly show how he can add the words found in this verse to the account in Deuteronomy 5 without admitting that the words *added no more* in Deuteronomy 5:22 really do not mean *added no more*. If anyone chooses to believe that the sabbath commandment existed before Sinai, he must get his evidence from a source other than Exodus 20 and Deuteronomy 5.

It is significant that the words "as the Lord commanded you" are found in the Deuteronomy 5 account of the Ten Commandments and not in the Exodus 20 account. This helps us establish exactly to what point in time Deuteronomy 5 refers. When did God 'command Israel' (the 'you' of verse 12) to keep the seventh day holy? Moses could not possibly be referring to Adam at creation because (1) Moses does not say, "commanded Adam" but "commanded you." (2) In Deuteronomy 5:2–3, Moses explicitly says, "the covenant (which included the Sabbath commandment) was not made with the *fathers,*" but was made at Sinai with those who came out of Egypt. This is why the reason given in Deuteronomy for obedience to the Sabbath is not referenced to Adam and Creation, but to Israel and their deliverance from Egypt. Adam could not have 'remembered the Exodus' as a reason for keeping the Sabbath, but the Israelites could. (3) Nowhere in Genesis does God command Adam, or anyone else, to keep the seventh day holy; but in Exodus 16:23-29, God did command, for the first time, Israel to keep the seventh day holy. (4) It would have been impossible for anyone to remember the redemption from Egypt before that redemption actually took place.

Three: The theological view of 'unchanging moral law' is greatly affected by having "two versions" of that law. As mentioned earlier, we must ask this question: "If God intended the tables of stone to be a revelation of his 'one unchanging moral law,' would he have given us *two different versions* of what he had written?" We think this is self-contradictory. We need to develop a new mindset that thinks and speaks in *biblical terms* instead of *theological terms*. Instead of accepting theological terms as if they were equal to Scripture verses, we need to insist on clear texts of Scripture. The Bible does not refer to the Ten Commandments as the 'unchanging moral law of God'; we must not do so either. Instead, we must begin to think and speak of them in a biblical manner. We must call them, as the writers of Scripture do, the 'tables of the covenant' or use one of the other biblical synonyms. Whenever we hear the words, 'the Ten Commandments', our first thought should automatically be, 'the terms of the Old Covenant written on the tables of stone at Mount Sinai.' Until we train ourselves to do this, we are not thinking and speaking in biblical terms.

We are not suggesting that there are no timeless duties written on the tablets of stone. The Ten Commandments contain much that is just as binding on a Christian today as it was on Moses and the Israelites. However, that is decidedly different from the concept that "the Ten Commandments, as written on the tablets of stone, are **THE eternal unchanging moral Law of God.**" We do not hesitate to say, "The Ten Commandments, not as written as a unit on the tablets of the covenant at Mount Sinai, but as *individually interpreted and applied by our Lord and his apostles in the New Covenant Scriptures,* are a very *essential part* of our rule of life."

We simply must fix in our minds that the Bible always treats the Ten Commandments as a single unit, or codified list, that constitutes a covenant document. When that covenant ended, everything it represented also ended. However, the specific duties commanded in the individual commandments written on those tables are another thing altogether. Nine of the ten individual commandments are clearly repeated as duties enjoined upon his followers by both our Lord in the Gospels and the apostles in the Epistles.

Every law that God commands is an 'ethical absolute' and is a 'duty' to the individual so commanded. To pick up sticks on the sabbath day was one of the most severely punished sins that a man could commit under the Old Covenant. Was his act of picking up sticks 'immoral'? What is inherently immoral about picking up a few sticks? In no sense is picking up sticks in and of itself an 'immoral' act. In Numbers 15:32-36, the man was stoned to death because the Fourth Commandment, which was the covenant sign, specifically forbade any physical labor on the seventh day. When viewed by itself, this commandment would seem to be purely 'ceremonial' in nature; yet it became a 'moral' duty when God made it the sign of the covenant. We will say more about covenant signs in a later chapter.

It was not 'immoral' for a man to take a second wife under the same Old Covenant that had a man stoned to death for gathering sticks. The same 'book of the covenant' (Exod. 24:7) that commanded 'keep the sabbath holy' also *commanded* a man to sleep with *both wives* when he took the *second one* (Exod. 21:10). Can anyone seriously believe that God would command a man to commit adultery for any reason whatsoever? Is it not easier to just believe what is clear in Scripture, namely, that polygamy was not a sin for an Israelite living under the Old Covenant? The exact opposite is true of the above two examples under the New Covenant. The Fourth Commandment established the sabbath as the ceremonial sign of the Old Covenant. The sign of the covenant ceased when the covenant, of which it was a sign, was done away in Christ (Col. 2:16-17; Heb. 8:13). The Seventh Commandment was changed by Christ and raised to a higher level by the new lawgiver. Although we have no specific text that states Polygamy is now a sin, a case can be built from the clear implications of texts like Ephesians 5:22-33 and 1 Corinthians 7. I think we can say, "Polygamy is now considered adultery." Polygamy was not a sin against the so-called 'moral law of God' according to the covenant under which David lived, but it is a sin according to the New Covenant under which a Christian lives today. Under the Old Covenant, picking up sticks on the sabbath was punishable by death. There is no holy twenty-four hour day under the New Covenant. The Bible defines a believer's duty according to the laws of the specific covenant under which that individual lives, and never by an imaginary code of 'unchanging moral law.'

Summary

The fact that there are *two conflicting versions* of the Ten Commandments in the Bible presents some problems. It would seem that there was less written on the tables of stone than most people realize. The Exodus 20 version and the Deuteronomy 5 version give two different accounts of the Fourth (Sabbath) Commandment. It seems impossible to us that God meant for us to think of the Ten Commandments as the 'eternal, unchanging moral law of God' when we are not positively sure what those commandments actually say. An Israelite's prescribed duty to God was not the same as that given to a Christian today. The Christian's duty is much higher because of grace (Heb. 12:25-29). An act that may not be inherently immoral may become a heinous sin under the terms of a given covenant.

Chapter Four

The Ten Commandments Are a 'Covenant' Document

The Scriptures, in some passages, clearly call the tablets of stone, or Ten Commandments, a covenant and treat them as a distinct covenant document. We have already seen this spelled out clearly in several texts of Scripture. However, despite the abundant textual evidence in the Scriptures for this fact, some theologians still cannot admit that the Ten Commandments are a covenant document. Their basic presupposition that there is only 'one covenant with two administrations' makes it impossible for them to think or speak of the Ten Commandments as a distinct, separate, and totally different covenant document. To do so would destroy the very foundation of their system of theology. In that system, the 'Mosaic arrangement' or 'Mosaic administration'[10] could not possibly be a separate covenant document, especially a *legal* covenant document. The 'Mosaic transaction,' a favorite expression used by Covenant Theologians, has to be an 'administration of the one covenant of grace.' However, the Word of God is quite clear that the Ten Commandments were the specific legal terms of a distinct legal covenant document. Here are several verses that clearly establish this point:

*So He declared to you His **covenant** which He **commanded you to perform,** that is, the **Ten Commandments;** and He wrote them on two **tablets of stone.** (Deut. 4:13 NASB)*

*When I went up on the mountain to receive the **tablets of stone,** the **tablets of the covenant** that the LORD had made with you ...The LORD gave me **two stone tablets** inscribed by the finger of God*

---

[10] These expressions are used by theologians who cannot or will not use biblical terminology for this particular point of doctrine. Whenever a writer is unable to use 'Mosaic *covenant'* and instead applies words like 'arrangement', 'administration', and 'transaction' to describe what happened at Sinai, it would appear that his theological creed and its particular terminology has become more important to him than the specific words inspired and used by the Holy Spirit himself.

*...the two stone tablets, the **tablets of the covenant.*** (Deut.9:9-11 NIV)

> *Then the LORD said to Moses, "Write down these words, for **in accordance with these words** I have made a **covenant** with you and with Israel." Moses was there with the LORD forty days and forty nights without eating bread or drinking water. And he wrote on the **tablets** the **words of the covenant--the Ten Commandments.*** (Exod. 34:27, 28 NIV)

Is it possible to read the above verses and, being honest with the words used, deny that the Ten Commandments were the very words, or terms, of a distinct and specific covenant document? A system of theology built on non-biblical terms and refusing to use biblical terms should be suspect. When a person uses terms that are peculiar and essential to his particular system of theology we should be wary of both the man and his system.

It is impossible even to begin to understand the place and function of the Ten Commandments in redemptive history until we begin where God's Word itself begins. We must start by using the terminology that the Holy Spirit has been pleased to use. When we do this, we will automatically think and speak of the Ten Commandments primarily as a distinct *covenant* document. If our theological system forbids that, or even makes it unnatural or difficult, then it should be obvious that our system is not biblical at that point.

The emphasis in the Word of God is always on the fact that the tablets of stone contain the terms of a covenant.

In chapter 1, we established that the Bible treats the *Ten Commandments,* the *tablets of the covenant,* and the *words of the covenant* as equivalent and interchangeable terms. It is clear from all of the biblical texts quoted in that chapter that God wants us to think *covenant* when there is a reference to either the words 'Ten Commandments' or any of the five synonymous terms used to describe them. To think of the Ten Commandments as something separate from the 'words of the covenant' written on the tablets of stone is to think non-biblically. Nowhere in the Bible are we instructed to think of the Ten Commandments in terms of *the eternal, unchanging moral law.* Review the biblical texts that refer to the Ten Commandments and see how clearly this truth is set forth in every text. This principle is not limited to the original tablets; it is just as striking when the second set was made after the first were smashed. It is not possible for the Bible to state any more clearly that the Ten Commandments are the exact words, or terms, of a covenant than it does in the following verses:

> *When Moses approached the camp and saw the calf and the dancing, his anger burned and he threw the **tablets** out of his hands, breaking them in pieces...*(Exod. 32:19 NIV)

> *The LORD said to Moses, "Chisel out two **stone tablets like the first ones,** and I will write on them the **words that were on the first tablets,** which you broke."... Then the LORD said: "I am making a COVENANT with you."... Then the LORD said to Moses, "Write down these words, for in accordance with them I have made a COVENANT with you and with Israel."... And he wrote on the **tablets the words of the COVENANT—the TEN COMMANDMENTS.*** (Exod. 34:1, 10, 27, 28 NIV)

Summary

The concept of the Ten Commandments as a covenant document is not a series of theological *deductions* derived from my particular system of theology; it is a statement of biblical fact. It is demonstrated in the texts of Scripture that we just covered. The *Bible teaches* that the Ten Commandments are a *distinct* and *specific covenant document!* The *Bible teaches* that the Ten Commandments are the terms of the Old Covenant! The *Bible uses* the terms 'Ten Commandments', 'tables of stone', 'tablets of testimony', 'words of the covenant', and 'tablets of the covenant' as interchangeable terms. *According to the Bible,* all of these terms mean exactly the same thing. I found the basis for each one of the statements in the previous paragraph in specific *Bible verses.* Not a single phrase or statement in that paragraph is 'deduced' from theology. If our theological system cannot agree with the explicit terms and statements used by the Holy Spirit himself, it is time to discard our theological system.

If our system of theology did not teach us to think about the Ten Commandments as a distinct and separate covenant document, then it did not teach us to think scripturally! If we were taught to think of the tablets of stone as the 'unchanging moral law of God', then we were taught to think only in theological terms that were created by men. Regrettably, we also were taught, by default, to ignore the words and terms used by the Holy Spirit himself. We may have done it unconsciously, but we nonetheless substituted theological words in the place of biblical words. Even worse, if we were taught that the Ten Commandments simply *could not be* a separate distinct covenant document, but only a different *administration* of the so-called Covenant of Grace, then we were taught to actually contradict the very words found in the Word of God when those words would not fit our system. We ought to seriously examine our theological system if that system cannot accept and use the clear biblical terms used by the Holy Spirit himself. If our theology cannot accept the fact that the Holy Spirit *always* connects the Ten Commandments, when considered as a unit, with the 'words of the covenant' that were written on the tablets of stone at Mount Sinai, then something is wrong with our theology.

Chapter Five

The Ten Commandments Are a 'Legal', or 'Works', Covenant Document

The tablets of stone, upon which God wrote the Ten Commandments, were not only a distinct and summary covenant document; they were the specific legal covenant document that established Israel as a special nation before God at Mount Sinai. The ark of the covenant establishes the fact that the Ten Commandments were the specific document that summarized the legal covenant terms that were the basis of God's special relationship with the nation of Israel. The Ten Commandments were the actual 'words of the covenant' that God made with Israel at Sinai. Exodus 34:27, 28; Deuteronomy 4:13 and other passages clearly state this fact. The Ten Commandments were kept in the ark of the covenant precisely because they were the summary covenant document that established and maintained Israel's special status before God.

The very name of the box that housed the Ten Commandments and the special care given to that box clearly demonstrate the true significance of the tablets of the covenant, the Ten Commandments. Nowhere does the Word of God even hint that the significance of the ark of the covenant was that it housed the so-called eternal, unchanging moral law of God. It housed the Old Covenant document that established Israel as a special nation before God and spelled out the major terms (the Ten Commandments) of that relationship, or covenant. That box was not the 'ark of the *moral law*.' It was the 'ark of the *covenant*' and the terms of the covenant were the Ten Commandments written on the tablets of the covenant and kept in the ark.

The importance that Scripture attaches to the Ten Commandments is always, without a single exception, connected with Israel's special status before God as a unique nation.

Several verses of Scripture emphasize this point clearly. One of the most important sections of Scripture in any discussion of the Ten Commandments is Exodus 19 through 24. Exodus 19 contains the preamble to the oral transmission of the Ten Commandments, recorded in Exodus 20. Exodus 24 records the official ratification of the book of the covenant with the sealing of blood. The writers of one particular school of theological thought emphasize the 'grace' shown by God in delivering Israel from bondage in Egypt (Exod. 19:3, 4), but seem to ignore the next two verses:

> 'Now *if you obey me fully and keep my covenant,* **then** *out of all nations you will be my treasured possession. Although the whole earth is mine, you will be for me a kingdom of priests and a holy nation.'* *These are the words you are to speak to the Israelites.* (Exod. 19:5, 6 NIV)

It is true that God showed special favor to the Jews in their redemption from Egypt, but that was a *physical redemption.* Most of those Israelites were still hard-hearted sinners who needed to be convinced of their lost estate (Heb. 3:16-19). God did **not** give the Ten Commandments to a 'redeemed [regenerate] people for their sanctification.' Such a view is not tenable simply because most of those people were not *regenerate believers.* God gave the Ten Commandments as a *legal covenant of life and death* to a nation composed of a mix of mostly proud sinners and a few regenerate believers as a means of driving the former to faith in the gospel preached to Abraham. As we shall see later, the primary function and goal of the Ten Commandments was a ministry of death by means of convicting the conscience of guilt.

We must not confuse the gracious *purpose* of God in giving the covenant at Sinai with the *nature* of the covenant itself. There was not an ounce of grace in the covenant itself, but it was very gracious of God to give the covenant to Israel. It was the necessary instrument to bring conviction of sin and lead to salvation by faith in the gospel preached to Abraham. By convicting of sin, the tablets of stone functioned in the conscience as a ministration of death; they could only do this if they had the status of a covenant with the power of life and death. Sinai was indeed the *handmaid* of the gospel of grace, but we must not confuse it with the gospel of grace itself.

John Owen is the exception to most writers in the Reformed tradition. He saw clearly that the Ten Commandments constituted a legal covenant document that was totally devoid of grace. He is one of the few writers (John Bunyan is another one) that knew how to separate law and grace. Some folks accuse us of 'misrepresenting Owen' when we use the following quotation. In no way whatever are we suggesting that John Owen was a New Covenant Theologian. That would indeed be a misrepresentation. However, we are claiming, and proving beyond question, that Owen's twofold definition of the word 'law' in the following quotations is exactly what we believe about the meaning of 'law.' These quotations are taken from a sermon on Romans 6:14 entitled, "You are not under the law, but under grace" which was published by his wife after Owen's death. It was one of the last things he wrote.

> The law is taken two ways: 1: For the **whole revelation of God in the Old Testament.** In this sense it had grace in it, and so did give both life, and light, and strength against sin, as the Psalmist declares, Ps. 19:79. In this sense it contained not only the law of precepts, but the promise also and strength unto the church. In this sense it is **not** spoken of here, [JGR: *i.e.* in Romans 6:14] nor is anywhere **opposed to grace.** 2: For the **covenant rule** of perfect obedience: 'Do this, and live.' In this sense men are said to be 'under it,' **in opposition** unto being '**under grace.**' They are under its power, rule, conditions and authority, as a **covenant.**[11]

Owen clearly saw that there was grace in 'the law' when 'law' is understood as the Old Testament *Scriptures* but there was no grace in 'the law' when it is viewed as the terms of the Old Covenant. The Old Covenant was a legal/works covenant. The tablets of the covenant established the conditions of the covenant

---

[11] John Owen, *The Works of John Owen* (Edinburgh: Banner of Truth, 1965), 7:542.

as *Do and live, disobey and die without mercy* (Heb. 10:28). Israel was 'under the law' as a covenant of life and death in the sense of Owen's second definition of the law. He calls it "The **covenant rule** of perfect obedience." Owen is following Paul when he acknowledges the distinct contrast between the covenant given to Israel and the covenant given to the church. He clearly communicated this in the last two sentences of the above quotation. Israel was 'under law' as opposed to 'under grace.' They were under the tablets of stone as a covenant, and that means, as Owen shows, that they were "under its power, rule, conditions, and authority, as a **covenant.**"

Owen boldly states that there was not an ounce of grace in the law when it is viewed as the legal covenant given to the nation of Israel at Sinai:

> *Fourthly,* **Christ is not in the Law;** he is not proposed in it, not communicated by it, we are not made partakers of him thereby. This is the work of grace, of the gospel. In it is Christ revealed; by it he is proposed and exhibited unto us … [12]

If that statement either shocks or confuses us, we have not yet understood the biblical doctrine of law and grace. We have not apprehended the nature, purpose, and function of the Ten Commandments as a covenant document. We have failed to see that God gave the tablets of stone to Israel as a ministration of death. That covenant document was meant to push men to faith in the gospel preached to Abraham. Neither Christ nor the gospel are found in the terms of *do and live, disobey and die*—and these were the specific covenant terms set forth at Sinai on the tablets of the covenant. It was these terms that the Israelites pledged themselves to obey upon pain of death. It was Israel's disobedience to these covenant terms that caused their captivities and final national rejection.

Many Reformed writers will emphasize the gracious act of God in *physically* redeeming Israel out of Egypt, but totally ne-

---

[12] Ibid. 551.

glect the fact that God immediately put Israel under a *conditional legal* covenant at Sinai. This is perplexing, especially when it is so clear in the Scripture. It is just as clear that the basic terms of this conditional legal covenant were nothing less than the tablets of the covenant upon which the Ten Commandments were written. Notice how clearly the following texts of Scripture show this truth in the 'if/then' nature of this conditional covenant:

> *Ye have seen what I did unto the Egyptians, and how I bare you on eagles' wings, and brought you unto myself* [It was indeed very gracious of God to physically deliver Israel from bondage]. *Now therefore,* **IF ye will obey** *my voice indeed, and* **keep my covenant,** **THEN ye shall be** *a peculiar treasure unto me above all people:* [Israel never became the true people of God simply because she never kept these covenant terms] *for all the earth is mine: and ye shall be unto me a kingdom of priests, and an holy nation. These are the words which thou shalt speak unto the children of Israel.* (Exod. 19:4-6)

It seems impossible to make the 'if/then' relationship in this text to be anything other than a legal covenant that promises certain blessings as a reward for obedience to the covenant terms. The special national status of Israel was based on the Ten Commandments as a covenant document; the covenant was conditional; it was a legal/works covenant that promised life and threatened death. As mentioned above, Israel never became the true holy nation. She was cast off without inheriting the blessings promised in the text. The church is the true 'holy nation,' or Israel of God, and all her members are 'kings and priests' (a kingdom of priests—See 1 Pet. 2-5:10). Christ, as the New Covenant Surety (Heb. 7:22), has kept the terms of the Old Covenant for his people and has earned every blessing it promised. When texts like Deuteronomy 7:6 speak of Israel as a 'holy nation' that had been 'chosen to be a special people' it does not mean they were a saved and sanctified people who had been chosen in Christ before the foundation of the world. They were indeed chosen, as a physical nation, out from all other nations, but that is not 'election unto salvation.' They were indeed redeemed by the blood of animals out of bondage to Egypt, but they were not redeemed by the blood of Christ and delivered out of bondage to sin. There were some truly saved individuals within the nation, but that was not the condition of most of the population. Hebrews 3:18–4:2 makes this clear.

Even a cursory comparison of Exodus 19:5, 6 with 1 Peter 2:9 will demonstrate that although both texts use the same words,[13] they are used in two different ways. These words refer to national Israel as a nation among nations and as such are 'God's special (national) people.' The same words also refer to the true Israel of God, or redeemed Body of Christ. Exodus 19 gives a list of the specific blessings that God promised Israel IF they would keep the covenant terms (the Ten Commandments). Israel never obeyed the terms of the covenant and therefore never received these blessings. She was finally cast off, as a nation, and lost her special national privileges. First Peter 2:9 shows that the church inherits those very blessings only because Christ has kept the covenant in her place. Notice the word-for-word comparison of Exodus and 1 Peter:

Exodus 19:5, 6 (KJV)	1 Peter 2:9 (NIV)
*Now therefore, IF ye will obey my voice indeed, and **keep my covenant, THEN ye shall be***	*But you **are** [because Christ kept the covenant for us]*
*(1) a **peculiar treasure** unto me above all people: for all the earth is mine: and ye shall be unto me*	*(1) a **chosen people**, ... a people belonging to God*
*(2) a **kingdom of priests**, and an*	*(2) a **royal** [kingly] **priesthood**,*
*(3) **holy nation**.*	*(3) a **holy nation**...*

---

[13] I have developed this point in detail in *The Four Seeds of Abraham*. This book examines the basic presuppositions of both Dispensationalism and Covenant Theology as they relate to the "*promise of God made to Abraham and his seed.*" It is available from New Covenant Media, 5317 Wye Creek Drive, Frederick, MD 21703-6938.

Both the beginning and the ending of Israel's special national standing and privileges are connected with their keeping or breaking the Ten Commandments.

The passage quoted above (Exodus 19:5, 6) certainly proves this point as to the institution of the nation. The termination of Israel's special national status proves the same thing. Israel's special national standing and privileges ended when the covenant ended that had established them as a nation. One of the most important verses in the New Testament Scriptures, from either a Dispensational or a Covenantal point of view, is Matthew 27:51. It definitely marks the end of both a dispensation and a covenant arrangement. The blood of Christ ratified the New Covenant, thus nullifying the Old Covenant, the moment Christ 'gave up the ghost' and died on the Cross. The entire theocratic kingdom established at Sinai ended at the same moment. Both of these things happened the moment the finger of God rent the veil of the temple from top to bottom. The way into the Most Holy Place is now open to all believers twenty-four hours a day. The same God who wrote that first covenant in stone with his finger now writes a new message with the same finger as he tears the veil and opens his immediate presence to all who come. The first covenant said, "Do not come near or even touch this mountain or you die," but the New Covenant that takes its place says, "Come and welcome, the door is wide open." The change of covenants makes the difference in the following texts:

> *The LORD said to Moses, "Tell your brother Aaron **not to come** whenever he chooses into the **Most Holy Place** behind the curtain in front of the atonement cover on the ark, or else he will die...*" Lev. 16:2 (NIV)

> *Therefore, brothers, since we have **confidence** to enter the **Most Holy Place** by the blood of Jesus, by a **new and living way**... Let us draw near...in full assurance...* Heb. 10:19- 22 (NIV)

At the very moment that the veil was rent, Israel's national status and privileges were ended,[14] along with everything that was connected to that special covenant relationship. Aaron's priesthood was finished, the sacrifices were done, the tabernacle was no longer holy, and the tables of the covenant (Ten Commandments) in the ark of the covenant were no longer in force as the covenant foundation of God's relationship to Israel. A 'better covenant', based on 'better promises' (Heb. 8:6), replaced the tablets of stone. The 'moment' described by Matthew is the exact moment that the decisive historical shift from the Old Covenant to the New Covenant took place.

> *And when Jesus cried out again with a loud voice, he gave up his spirit.* ***At that moment*** *the curtain of the temple was torn in two from top to bottom. The earth shook and the rocks split.* (Matt. 27:50, 51 NIV)

The change of status brought into being by the change of covenants was a truth despised by the Jews. The words, "There is no difference" killed every ounce of pride in their birth, their circumcision, and their exclusive possession of the law. Two things happened with the coming of the kingdom of grace. First, the Gentile believer was made an equal heir with the Jewish believer in the one new man (Eph. 2:14-16), or body of Christ, and secondly, the unbelieving Jew was reduced to the same level and status before God as the unbelieving Gentile dog. Before Christ came, there was a great difference in privileges between Jew and Gentile (see Ephesians 2 and Romans 9), but once the Body of Christ came into being at Pentecost, and Judaism in its totality was ended, there was no difference at all. Just as all believers have the same status 'in Christ,' all lost people have the same status 'outside of Christ.'

---

[14] I believe the Scripture makes a clear distinction between Israel as a 'nation' and Israel as an 'ethnic people.' The first is finished but the second is not. For a clear presentation of ethnic Israel's hope for the future, see John Murray, *The New International Commentary on the New Testament; The Epistle to the Romans,* Vol II (Grand Rapids, MI., Wm. B. Eerdman's Publishing Co., 1977) pp 65-90

Every attempt to hang on to that which was distinctive of the Old Covenant and antithetical to the New Covenant was a further display of the Jews' rejection of Christ as the Messiah. The Jewish nation not only rejected the *message* spoken by Christ, they also dismissed one of the greatest *object lessons* that God ever gave. We do not know if they sewed that old veil back together or made a new one, but regardless, in re-hanging that veil they disavowed every promise God had fulfilled and earned every judgment their own prophets had clearly foretold. The times of the Messiah and the gospel blessing to *all people* that had been promised in the Abrahamic covenant had finally come. However, the Jewish nation could not believe the truth. 'There is *no difference*' could not penetrate the blind eyes and proud heart of the formerly favored Jew.

With the rending of the veil, the Most Holy Place was not the only area of the tabernacle that was finished; there was no longer a separate Court of Gentiles. Paul sets forth the heart of this truth in Romans 2 and 3; 9:1-18; 10:1-13; Ephesians 2:11-21; and Galatians 3:19-4:7.

The Ten Commandments, or tablets of stone, constituted the actual covenant document that established Israel as a nation.

Many details were added to the 'covenant' that explained and applied the covenant terms written on the tablets of the covenant to diverse areas of life and worship. The entire section of Exodus 20-22 is called the 'book of the covenant.' The law of Moses included everything in the Pentateuch, and as such, was sometimes called 'the law' or 'the covenant.' Perhaps we could think of the tables of the covenant as a summary document that stood for the whole covenant arrangement, in the same way as a covenant sign stood for the whole covenant. Regardless, we must still see that the tablets of stone, or Ten Commandments, were a special covenant document that established Israel's nationhood in the same sense that the Constitution of the United States is the covenant document that established it as a nation. The acts of Congress, the decisions of the Supreme Court, the rules of the IRS, Food and Health department laws, etc., are all part of the 'law of the United States of America' just as the judicial, ceremonial, social, and health laws are all part of the 'law of Moses.' However, the Constitution is still the specific and separate document upon which all else rests. The same is true of the tablets of the covenant, or the Ten Commandments.

All of the laws of the various departments in our government grow out of the Constitution. They define and apply specific sections of the Constitution to given situations. However, the fact remains that the actual **covenant document** upon which our nationhood was established, and by which we still are governed, is the Constitution. In the same sense, the Ten Commandments written on the tablets of stone were the 'words of the covenant' that constituted the basic **covenant foundation** of Israel's special nationhood before God. A chart of comparison may help us to understand this point:

Covenant Document	Covenant Document
Ten Commandments	The Constitution
Laws in the book of the Covenant	Laws of Congress
Judges	Supreme Court
Civil and Social Laws	Justice Department
Health Laws	Department of Health
Tithing Laws	Department of Welfare
"The law of Moses"	"The law of the USA"

Summary

The preceding chart emphasizes the main points we are seeking to establish. The Ten Commandments are indeed a covenant document that set forth specific covenant terms. They function as a 'foundation document' in the same manner as the Constitution of the United States. In the United States, diverse agencies with specific laws were created to direct various aspects of the lives of American citizens living under the constitution; in the same manner, Israel had assorted laws to govern various aspects of her life under her covenant. We must avoid two mistakes. First, just as the Constitution of the United States does not contain the whole law of its government, so the Ten Commandments are not the 'whole law of God' for Israel. Second, we must not deny that both the Constitution and the tables of the covenant, the Ten Commandments, are basic covenant documents upon which each respective nation was built.

The primary resistance to consideration of the Ten Commandments as a legal covenant document is that such a view cannot be squared with the tenet of a "Covenant of Works with Adam before he fell and a Covenant of Grace with Adam after he fell." Within such a framework, there can be no Covenant of Works after Adam 'failed to earn life' under the so-called Covenant of Works in Eden. Nor can there ever be another Covenant of Works once the so-called Covenant of Grace has been established. The 'transaction' at Sinai must be turned into 'an administration of the Covenant of Grace' or the whole system is destroyed. Mount Sinai simply cannot be a legal covenant if a 'Covenant of Works/Covenant of Grace with Adam' concept is accepted.

Chapter Six

The Ten Commandments, as Covenant Terms, Were Given Only to the Nation of Israel

The Old Testament Scriptures repeatedly state that the covenant terms written on the tablets of stone were made only with Israel. We saw this truth in chapter 1 when we looked at the first occurrence of the words 'Ten Commandments' in the Bible. The Scripture is quite clear that the Ten Commandments, as a covenant document, were given only to the nation of Israel:

> And the LORD said unto Moses, Write thou **these words:** for after the **tenor of these words** I have made a **covenant** with thee and **WITH ISRAEL.** And he was there with the LORD forty days and forty nights; he did neither eat bread, nor drink water. And he wrote upon the tables the **words of the covenant, the ten commandments.** (Exod. 34:27, 28)

When Moses refreshed Israel's mind concerning their covenant relationship with God, he specifically stated that the covenant (Ten Commandments) was given to Israel alone at Horeb. This is clear in the following text:

> The LORD our God **made a covenant** [Remember the covenant terms are the **Ten Commandments** or tablets of stone] with **us at Horeb.** The LORD did **not** make **this covenant** with **our fathers,** but with **us,** with all those of **us** alive here today. (Deut. 5:2, 3 NASB)

Moses insists that the covenant was "**not** made with our fathers," meaning the patriarchs,[15] but with the people that came out of Egypt. He then repeats the words of the covenant, or Ten Commandments, that God wrote on the tablets of the covenant at Sinai.

---

[15] The writer of Hebrews, as well as the prophecy in Jeremiah 31:33, establishes beyond question that the 'fathers' referred to in this passage are the patriarchs. To make the statement refer to the immediate fathers of the people to whom Moses is speaking would involve a contradiction. It was specifically to these immediate 'fathers,' as opposed to the patriarchs who lived prior to the giving of the law, that God gave the covenant at Sinai.

The prophets saw the coming of a New Covenant and spoke of it in glowing terms. Whenever they contrasted the Old Covenant with the New Covenant, they always stated *when* and *with whom* the Old Covenant was made. Notice this in the classic passage in Jeremiah:

> *Behold, days are coming, declares the LORD, when I will make a **new covenant** with the house of Israel ...not like the **covenant** which I made with **their fathers** in the day I took them by the hand **to bring them out of the land of Egypt** ...*(Jer. 31:31, 32 NASB)

The following points are clearly set forth in this passage:

1. God said that he was going to make a new covenant.... "*I will make a **new covenant** ....*"

2. The New Covenant was going to be *different in nature* from the Old Covenant it replaced. "*... **not like the covenant** I made with their fathers....*"

3. The Old Covenant being replaced was made at Sinai and made only with Israel. "*...made with their fathers **in the day** I took them by the hand to bring them out of **the land of Egypt**...*"

How is it possible to read these words in Jeremiah and say, "God was not actually promising to make a new and different *covenant* with Israel; he was really promising a new *administration* of the *same covenant* they were already under"? It seems to me that such statements contradict what Jeremiah said. The rest of the Bible concurs with Jeremiah when it speaks on this subject. The following passage from 1 Kings appears to be going out of its way to affirm the facts we are setting forth:

> *There was nothing in the ark save the two tables of stone, which Moses put there at Horeb, **WHEN** the LORD made a covenant with the children of Israel, **WHEN** they came out of the land of Egypt.* (1 Kings 8:9)

The phrases *tables of stone, Moses at Horeb, made a covenant,* and *children of Israel* in this text are the same key ingredients that we always find connected with the Ten Commandments.

This passage of Scripture uses the word 'when' two times. We could put a period after 'children of Israel' and not lose the thought or argument. The last phrase in the sentence, "*When* they came out of the land of Egypt," is almost redundant. The Holy Spirit must have wanted to impress this point on our minds.

The New Testament Scriptures always connect the Old Covenant, or Ten Commandments, with Israel alone.

Hebrews 8:8-9 is the inspired apostolic interpretation of Jeremiah 31:31, 32. There is no question in the mind of the writer of Hebrews concerning: (1) *when* the Old Covenant was made; (2) *with whom* the Old Covenant was made; (3) or the fact the New Covenant would be *different* than the Old Covenant. The passage is clear:

> *...the time is coming, declares the Lord, when I will make a **new covenant** with the **house of Israel** ...It will **not be like the covenant** I made with their forefathers **when** I took them by the hand to **lead them out Egypt...*** (Heb. 8:8, 9 NIV)

I do not wish to belabor a clearly established fact or beat a dead horse. However, I simply cannot understand how sincere people who believe in the *verbal* inspiration of the Bible can refuse to accept and use the *words* that the Holy Spirit inspired and used. Let the reader judge for himself: (1) Did God specifically promise to make a new *covenant,* or did he promise a new *administration* of the *same* covenant? (2) Was the Old Covenant made with *Israel* at Sinai or was it made with *Adam* in the Garden? What does Scripture say? The great difference between the nation of Israel and the Gentiles was that of 'having the law' as a covenant and the gospel as a promise, as opposed to 'not having the law' and being without a covenant or hope (Ephesians 2:11-21).

The following text is a key passage on this particular point:

> *For when the Gentiles, **which have not the law,** do by nature the things contained in the law, these, **having not the law,** are a law unto themselves: Which shew the **work of the law** written in their hearts, their **conscience** also bearing witness...* (Rom. 2:14)

The word 'law' in this passage has to refer to the tablets of stone as a covenant document. It cannot refer only to 'conscience' since Paul has already established in chapter 1 that all men (Jew and Gentile) are without excuse, and earlier in chapter 2 has determined that any man (Jew or Gentile) who exercises moral judgment of another person is himself then subject to judgment. All men have some sense of ethical duty. Paul is talking about a law that some men definitely *do not have.* Furthermore, if all men, Jew and Gentile alike, do indeed 'have the law' in the sense that Paul uses the word in this passage, his argument still does not make sense. He is contradicting himself. Paul's point in the context of this passage is to show that the Jews are guiltier than the Gentiles. The basis of his proof is that the Gentiles '*without* the law' live better lives than the Jews do '*with* the law.' The Jews alone have the special gift of the law as a covenant document. And the specific law that he is talking about is the law written on the tablets of stone as covenant terms. This is an example of the tables of the testimony, or Ten Commandments, being used as a witness against Israel to show her greater guilt.

In Romans 2:14, Paul cannot be talking about a so-called ceremonial law. Whatever the law is in this passage, it convicts the conscience of sin. Conscience, by nature and without special revelation, cannot convict men of disobedience to 'ceremonial' laws. One evidence that the sabbath is not of the same nature as the other nine commandments is that we have never discovered a single instance of anyone knowing, by nature, the seventh-day sabbath law given to Israel alone. That particular law must always be taught as special revelation, just as it was to Israel at Sinai.[16] Pagans intuitively know that adultery is wrong and they

---

[16] John Bunyan wrote an excellent article proving the seventh-day sabbath could not possibly be a "Creation Ordinance." To my knowledge, no one has attempted to answer his arguments. See, *The Works of John Bunyan,* (Grand Rapids, MI,) Baker Book House, 2:359 - 367. See also: John G. Reisinger, *The Believer's Sabbath* (Frederick, MD: New Covenant Media, 2002).

know they should worship God, but they never know a one-in-seven cycle or a holy seventh day until they are so instructed.

It is easy to misquote Romans 2:14. Paul does not say *the law* is written in the Gentiles' hearts, but the *work* of the law. The purpose of the law is to "work wrath" (Rom. 4:15). God gave it for that very purpose. However, it can only "work wrath" to the degree that the law, regardless of what specific law you are talking about, is known. Paul says that certain behavior proves there is a conviction of right and wrong in all men. This fact shows that the conscience is alive and doing its work even in the Gentiles. In fact, the conscience is more alive and well in them than it is in the Jew. This power of conscience "shows the *work* of the law written in their hearts." The 'work' of the law is to accuse and excuse according to the standard it reveals; it condemns all violations of known wrong and rewards obedience to what is known to be right. All men have a conscience and they all experience, to a greater or lesser degree, conviction they have done wrong or right in some instances.

Actually, Israel 'had the law' but they did *not* have the '*work* of the law' written in their hearts. Their consciences were seared. The Gentiles did *not* have 'the law' but they *did have* the '*work* of the law' in their hearts. The law can only 'work' and convict of guilt if the individual has knowledge of the terms of that law. In giving Israel the law as a covenant, God enlightened the mind and sharpened the conscience. He placed the conscience under the Old Covenant and its threat of judgment. This caused a very painful death to all hope of eternal life in those who truly experienced the end for which the law covenant was given, namely, genuine conviction of guilt. The same law actually 'blinded' the rest of the Jews in their self-righteousness and made them worse off spiritually than the Gentiles.

It was most *gracious* of God to give the law to kill Israel's hope in their own efforts. However, it took a covenant of law with the power of life and death to do the job. There was not an ounce of grace in the tablets of stone, but it was most gracious of

God to give them to Israel as a covenant document that could prepare the heart to receive grace!

Regardless of whether the reader agrees or disagrees with what has just been said, one thing is certain. We cannot change a passage of Scripture that emphatically states that Israel *had* a specific law that the Gentiles *did not have* into a text that says 'all men have the same law.' That would be to destroy the text. I see no way that Paul can be referring to anything but the tables of stone as a covenant document. However, this is in no way integral to the thesis of this book.

It both amazes and amuses me to watch people waver back and forth when they cannot fit clear passages of Scripture into their theological system. If the 'eternal, unchanging moral law' is under discussion, then adherents to Covenant Theology will insist that the moral law (Ten Commandments) is written on every man's heart. However, if the canon of conduct for believers today is the topic, these same people insist that, in regeneration, 'the moral law' (Ten Commandments) is written on the heart by the Holy Spirit. In both cases, it is said to be the *same law* that Scriptures clearly state was given *only* to the nation of Israel at Sinai on the tablets of stone.

Something seems to be a bit out of focus when all of these facets of Covenant Theology are put together. (1) If the first point is true, namely that the so-called 'moral law' is indeed the Ten Commandments, and that 'moral law' given to Israel at Sinai (the Ten Commandments) is indeed written on every man's heart, then it is impossible to say the Gentiles are 'without the law.' They cannot be without the very law that is written in them. (2) If the second point, affirming that the same law written in the heathen, and given to Israel at Sinai is also specifically written on the heart of believers in regeneration, is true, then there appears to be a contradiction. What need is there to write something on the heart that is already there? You may 'polish it up a bit,' but you cannot write something on the heart that is already there.

We must distinguish between the Ten Commandments as (1) the terms of a legal covenant document and (2) the duties commanded by the individual commandments: some fall into the realm of ethics, and at least one can easily be classified as ceremonial. When we make this distinction between a unified entity and individual commandments, much confusion disappears and some difficult passages of Scripture become clear and simple. We will illustrate this point with one passage of Scripture. This passage in its context is pivotal to a correct understanding of the change of covenants:

> But the ministry Jesus has received is as superior to theirs as the covenant of which he is mediator is superior to the old one, and it is founded on better promises. For if there had been nothing wrong with that first covenant, no place would have been sought for another. But God found fault with the people and said: "The time is coming, declares the Lord, when **I will make a new covenant** with the house of Israel and with the house of Judah. It will **not be like the covenant** I made with their forefathers when I took them by the hand to lead them out of Egypt, because they did not remain faithful to my covenant, and I turned away from them, declares the Lord. **This is the covenant I will make** with the house of Israel after that time, declares the Lord. **I will put my laws in their minds and write them on their hearts.** I will be their God, and they will be my people. No longer will a man teach his neighbor, or a man his brother, saying, 'Know the Lord,' because they will all know me, from the least of them to the greatest. For I will forgive their wickedness and will remember their sins no more." By calling this covenant "new," he has made the first one obsolete; and what is obsolete and aging will soon disappear. (Heb. 8:6-13 NIV)

We have already noted three distinct contrasts in verse 6. We saw the following: (1) Christ has a *better **ministry*** than Aaron, (2) because Christ's ministry is based on a new and *better **covenant.*** (3) The covenant Christ administers is superior to the covenant under which Aaron ministered because it is based on *better **promises.***

Verses 7-9 provide historical background and settle any discussion as to either *when* (at Sinai) or *with whom* (Israel only) the

Old Covenant was made. Verse 11 continues the distinctive contrasts and shows that everyone, without a single exception, in the New Covenant community, or church, 'knows the Lord.' In other words, the text proves that the church born under the New Covenant has a totally regenerate membership. The same could not be said of the nation born at Sinai. Verse 10 emphasizes several important concepts:

> *This is the **covenant** I will make with the **house of Israel** after that time, declares the Lord. I will put my **laws in their minds** and write them on **their hearts.** I will be their God, and they will be my people.* (Heb. 8:10 NIV)

First, God promises to make a new covenant, and this covenant will be with the "house of Israel." It is obvious that the promise, as stated in Jeremiah 33, refers to the nation of Israel. It is not, perhaps, as clear from the text in Hebrews that the church is included in the fulfillment of that promise. We owe our understanding of that truth to Paul's letter to the Ephesians. He plainly states, in 2:11-22, that Jew and Gentile alike now constitute one new man in Christ. They are one new dwelling where God lives by his Spirit, and their condition is united. Thus, by extension, a covenant made with one is made with all. The blood of Christ that makes one new man out of Jew and Gentile is the very blood that establishes the New Covenant (1 Cor. 11:25). This New Covenant cannot be made to apply to only Jewish people or pushed into a future millennium. The people of God are now one people, drawn from both the house of Israel and from the nations, and cannot be divided. The writer is not talking about the future but the present. One of the themes in Hebrews is the priestly ministry of Christ over the church. However, that is not our subject in this book.

The second major idea in the text is God's promise to put his laws in the mind and write them on the hearts of his New Covenant people. This raises the question: *What is the difference, if any, between the word **'covenant'** and the word 'laws' in this passage?* Exactly what is God promising to do in this verse? Exactly what is the 'New Covenant' he is making and precisely what laws is he going to write on the heart?

We should carefully note that God did *not* say, "In that day I will give a new and better *administration* of the *same covenant* that I gave Israel. I will write the old law of Sinai into the new heart of the Christian." That is how some theologians read this passage. Likewise, the text does *not* say, "I will make a New Covenant that destroys all of the Ten Commandments and allows a believer to do as he pleases." That is what some people are *accused* of saying. No, the text and its broader context are talking about *both* a new and better covenant than the Old Covenant at Sinai, and a new experience of "the law being written on the heart by the indwelling Spirit." If the Old Covenant believer had the same law, in the same sense, written on his heart that is written on the heart of a believer in regeneration under the New Covenant, then what is so great and different under the New Covenant? It seems all is the same under both covenants. The glory of the New Covenant has been lost.

The clear answers to these questions lie in understanding the three comparisons made in verse 6. Why did the Old Covenant fail and thereby need to be replaced by a new and better covenant? The answer is that the Old Covenant could not secure the necessary obedience to its terms. It could not write on the heart the *desire* to do the things that were written on the tablets of the covenant. It could write on stone but not on flesh (2 Cor. 3). By nature, every lost man hates God's authority (Rom. 8:7), and even the mighty law of God cannot change that rebellion into a sincere desire to obey. The Old Covenant failed to bring sinners into God's presence because it could not change the sinners' hearts. It could neither conquer sin in the flesh nor could it cleanse the conscience from the guilt of sin.

Heed this carefully! The greater glory of the New Covenant is *not* that the standards or laws have been lowered or removed. It is *not* that the morality that undergirded the duties demanded on the tables of stone is no longer binding on a Christian. The greater glory of the New Covenant is that the terms that must be met in order to come into God's presence require no obedience on our part at all. This is true simply because the very terms of the tablets of the covenant have been finally and fully met in the person and work of our surety, the Lord Jesus Christ. Our surety has both earned the very righteousness that the Old Covenant demanded and endured the awful curse of that same covenant against disobedience. The glory of the New Covenant is in the words, "IT IS FINISHED." Paul states the glory of the New Covenant in the classic passage in Romans 4:5. Carefully follow the words and an explanatory paraphrase of that text:

> *However, to the man who does not work* [by honoring Christ as the true sabbath] *but trusts God* [by ceasing to work for his standing with God and by faith alone enters into God's true rest in Christ] *who justifies the wicked, his faith is credited as righteousness.* (Rom. 4:5 NIV)

This is the 'rest' into which weary souls enter when they come under the yoke of Christ. It stands in sharp distinction to the yoke of the covenant given to Moses on Sinai. We doubt not that our Lord Jesus had this very contrast in mind when he gave that great gospel invitation in Matthew 11:28-30:

> *Come to **me**, all you who are weary and burdened, and **I will give you rest*** [I will sabbath your soul]. *Take **my yoke** upon you and **learn from me**, for I am gentle and humble in heart, and you will find **rest for your souls**. For **my yoke** is easy and my burden is light.* (Matt. 11:28-30 NIV)

Everything in that passage is a contrast with Moses and the old law covenant. The yoke of the covenant written on the tables of stone was a burden impossible to bear (Acts 15:10). The yoke written in the blood of Calvary is a privilege and delight to bear. The New Covenant is nothing less than Christ himself and his finished work. When God said, "I will make a New Covenant," he was saying, "I will give you Christ to be your covenant keeper. He will both keep the law and die under its curse." The message has now become 'It is finished' instead of 'Do or Die.'

The New Covenant, unlike the Old Covenant, is one of grace and not works.

What then are the specific laws spoken of in Hebrews 8:10? Exactly what laws does the Holy Spirit write on the heart of a New Covenant believer? Hebrews 8:10 is not presenting two different *sets* of laws that contradict each other as if there were two kinds of morality. The text presents two sets of parallels: "I will put my laws in their minds" is a *parallel contrast* to "No longer will a man teach his neighbor or a man his brother, saying, 'Know the Lord.'" The second set is a *parallel agreement*: "I will write them [my laws] on their hearts" compares to "they will all know me." The law written on the heart is knowledge of God. Knowledge of God is far more than mere recognition of his existence; it is love for all that he reveals himself to be.

The New Covenant does not start at square one, but builds on what God has already revealed in the Old Covenant. Thus, it does not 'throw away' the duties commanded on the tables of stone, but recognizes that the stone tables were a limited revelation. They could provide revelation that would result in recognition of God's character, but could not impart love for the God whose character they revealed. Christ reveals more of God than Moses ever could; Christ is the exact representation of God's being, while Moses only knew as much of God as God was pleased to reveal to him. Under the New Covenant, Christ adds laws that were impossible for Moses to ever give, but that does not mean Christ contradicts Moses.[17] It simply means that Christ speaks to hearts that love God. Hebrews compares two different *motivations* that grow out of two different kinds of *covenants*. The primary idea of 'writing the law on the heart' is that of a regenera-

---

[17] I have worked this out in detail in *But I Say Unto You*. This book shows that Christ supersedes and replaces Moses as the New Lawgiver in exactly the same way that he replaces Aaron as High Priest. Christ changes some of the laws of Moses; raises some others to a higher level; discards others altogether; and adds some laws that are new. However, this is not *contradicting* Moses as if he had been wrong. The book is available from New Covenant Media, 5317 Wye Creek Drive, Frederick, MD 21703-6938.

tion that gives a new heart that desires and is able to obey. The *content* of what is written is not the major point of contrast, but rather the *motivation*; the desire to obey from the heart.

Second Corinthians 3 is the Holy Spirit's commentary on Hebrews 8:10. Neither of these passages teaches that God tattoos the exact words of the Decalogue on our hearts. Both passages refer to the powerful effect of regeneration which results in a new and different attitude toward God. These two passages picture the removal of the stony heart that hated the tablets of stone and all they represented. They describe the effect of regeneration in replacing the stony heart with a heart of flesh. The new heart of flesh loves **all** of God's laws as they are revealed in Christ, not just one small code, simply because it loves the new lawgiver who teaches those laws.

The difference between the Old and New Covenants is not primarily in the specific duties demanded, but in the difference between law and grace as *covenants.* It is the difference, in some cases, of *identical duties* being enforced from *without* by fear and force, as is the case of the Old Covenant, and being constrained from *within* by love and a heart rejoicing in a covenant based on grace. These two passages present the difference between a conscience imprisoned under the old Pedagogue, the tables of stone, and a conscience set free under the new Pedagogue, the indwelling Holy Spirit.

Summary

It is clear from Scripture that the Ten Commandments, as a covenant document, were given only to the nation of Israel. The phrase "having the law" often is used to distinguish Israel from the Gentiles. The Gentiles, because they were not given the law, were "separate from Christ, excluded from citizenship in Israel and foreigners to the covenants of the promise, without hope and without God in the world" (Eph. 2:12 NIV).

The Old Covenant, which included the Ten Commandments, was a legal covenant based upon works as contrasted with the New Covenant based on the merits of Christ given to us entirely by grace. The basic difference between the Old and New Covenants has nothing to do with "two different kinds of laws" but the basis of blessing: law and works or grace and faith. The "law written on the heart" concerns the reality of a regenerated heart that loves and sincerely desires to keep all of God's will, as it is revealed in Christ. Every New Covenant believer experiences this blessing.

Chapter Seven

The Seventh-Day Sabbath Was the Sign of the Mosaic Covenant!

Because the tablets of stone/Ten Commandments were a distinct covenant document, a specific covenant sign accompanied them. I am aware that very few writers or preachers ever present the sabbath as the sign of the covenant written on the tablets of the covenant. However, it is not because the Word of God is not both clear and emphatic. One question that is nearly always asked when the sabbath is discussed goes something like this: "If the sabbath was not part of the 'moral law,' then why was it included on the tablets of stone as one of the Ten Commandments?" I wish every question I am asked was as easy to answer as this one. The sabbath was the *sign of the covenant* that God made with Israel and therefore it had to be *part of the covenant document of which it was the sign.* The answer is just that simple. It has nothing to do with 'moral' law.

The following texts teach not only that the sabbath was the sign of the covenant given at Sinai, but they show the great importance of the sabbath sign as well:

*And the LORD spake unto Moses, saying, Speak thou also unto the children of Israel, saying, Verily **my sabbaths** ye shall keep: for it is a **sign between me and you** throughout your generations; that ye may know that I am the LORD that doth sanctify you. Ye shall keep the sabbath therefore; for it is holy unto you: every one that defileth it shall surely be put to death: for whosoever doeth any work therein, that soul shall be cut off from among his people. Six days may work be done; but in the seventh is the sabbath of rest, holy to the LORD: whosoever doeth any work in the sabbath day, he shall surely be put to death. Wherefore the **children of Israel** shall keep **the sabbath,** to observe the sabbath throughout their generations, for a **perpetual covenant.** It is a **sign between me and the children of Israel for ever:** for in six days the LORD made heaven and earth, and on the seventh day he rested, and was refreshed. And he gave unto Moses, when he had made an end of communing with* *him upon mount Sinai, **two tables of testimony, tables of stone, written with the finger of God.*** (Exod. 31:12-18)

This text establishes five facts:

First, the Ten Commandments are synonymous with 'tables of stone' and the two 'tables of testimony.' They are the actual covenant document that established Israel's special national status with God. *"...two tables of **testimony,** tables of stone, written with the finger of God."*

Second, the sabbath, or Fourth Commandment, was the sign of the covenant. *"...the children of Israel shall keep the **sabbath**... for a perpetual **covenant.** It is a **sign** between me and the children of Israel forever..."*

Third, the sign of the covenant, or sabbath, stands for the whole covenant. To break the sign is to despise the entire covenant. *"...keep the sabbath ...for a perpetual **covenant.**"*

Fourth, the covenant was made only with the nation of Israel. *"...the **children of Israel** shall keep the sabbath ...It is a **sign** between me and the **children of Israel**..."*

Fifth, the essence of the sabbath commandment was to refrain from all physical work. It had nothing to do with public worship. *"...whosoever doeth **any work** ...Six days may **work be done,** but the seventh is the **sabbath of rest** ...whosoever doeth **any work** in the sabbath day, he shall surely be put to death."*

The following passage from Ezekiel is helpful at this point. It not only demonstrates that the sabbath was the sign of the covenant written on the tables of stone, it also shows that this particular commandment was so important only because it was the covenant's sign. Read the text carefully:

> *And I gave them my statutes, and shewed them my judgments, which if a man **DO,** he shall even **live in them.** Moreover also I gave them **my sabbaths, to be a sign** between me and them, that they might know that I am the LORD that sanctify them. But the house of Israel rebelled against me in the wilderness: they walked not in my statutes, and they despised my judgments, which if a man do, he*

shall even live in them; and **my sabbaths** *they greatly polluted:* **THEN** *I said, I would pour out my fury upon them in the wilderness, to consume them. But I wrought for my name's sake, that it should not be polluted before the heathen, in whose sight I brought them out. Yet also I lifted up my hand unto them in the wilderness, that I would not bring them into the land which I had given them, flowing with milk and honey, which is the glory of all lands; Because they despised my judgments, and walked not in my statutes, but polluted* **my SABBATHS:** *for their heart went after their idols. Nevertheless mine eye spared them from destroying them, neither did I make an end of them in the wilderness. But I said unto their children in the wilderness, Walk ye not in the statutes of your fathers, neither observe their judgments, nor defile yourselves with their idols: I am the LORD your God; walk in my statutes, and keep my judgments, and do them; And* **hallow my SABBATHS;** *and they shall be a* **SIGN between me and you,** *that ye may know that I am the LORD your God.* (Ezek. 20:11-20)

Notice the word 'then' in verse 13 and its connection to verses 16 and 20. Israel committed many grievous sins, but it was not until they 'profaned the sabbath' that they went into captivity. Again, this shows that breaking the sign of the covenant is equivalent to despising the whole covenant. To profane the sabbath would appear to be the worst possible sin that an Israelite could commit. Israel's Babylonian captivity was measured in terms of how many years they had refused to observe the sabbath-year law to let the land lie idle (cf. Jer. 29:10 and 2 Chron. 36:21). We may conclude from these texts that the most serious of the Ten Commandments, as far as it involved judgment, was the fourth, and that its importance lay solely in the fact that it was the sign of the covenant. The fact that the judgment that consisted of captivity for seventy years was for breaking the *sabbath-year law* shows that all of the sabbaths were just as holy as the seventh-day sabbath. Paul makes this clear in Colossians 2:14-17.

Colossians 2:16 is an important verse for several reasons. Everyone agrees that Paul is declaring that the "holy days, the new moon, and the sabbath" are all done away in Christ. However, the sabbatarian insists that Paul is not referring to the 'moral' seventh-day sabbath, but is referring only to the *ceremonial* sabbath*s* (plural). A careful reading of the passage clearly proves that Paul includes the weekly seventh-day sabbath as one of the 'shadows' that are fulfilled and done away in Christ. Let us look at the verse and its context:

> And you, being dead in your sins and the uncircumcision of your flesh, hath he quickened together with him, having forgiven you all trespasses; Blotting out the handwriting of ordinances that was against us, which was contrary to us, and took it out of the way, nailing it to his cross; And having spoiled principalities and powers, he made a show of them openly, triumphing over them in it. Let no man therefore judge you in meat, or in drink, or in respect of an holyday, or of the new moon, or of the sabbath days: Which are a shadow of things to come; but the body is of Christ. (Col. 2:13-17)

It is crucial to note in verses 16 and 17 that Paul emphatically states that the shadows, consisting of holy days, the new moon, and the sabbaths, are done away because the body, or the fulfillment of those things, has come in the person and work of Christ. As mentioned above, the point in question is whether Paul includes the seventh-day sabbath or only refers to so-called ceremonial sabbaths. Can the passage sustain an 'only ceremonial sabbaths' interpretation, or does it clearly include the seventh-day sabbath with those done away under the New Covenant?

Verse 13 makes it clear that the apostle is talking about regeneration and salvation ("you hath he quickened"—God made you alive with Christ). Verse 14 shows that the forgiveness of sins in salvation came only because "the handwriting of ordinances that was against us, which was contrary to us" has been "taken out of the way" by being "nailed to his cross." The law that was nailed to the Cross is the same law that stood between God and us.[18] It was the nailing of that law to the Cross, or Jesus dying under its curse, that brought eternal salvation to God's people. Jesus did not bear

---

[18] Paul's deliberate change of pronouns from *you* to *us* is as important here as it is in Galatians 3 and 4.

the curse of a so-called ceremonial law. That is not the law that stood against us or that was nailed to the Cross.

The "handwriting of ordinances" in these verses can only be a description of the tables of the testimony (Exod. 31:18; 34:27-29), or the Ten Commandments. They are called tables of *testimony* because, as the terms of the Old Covenant, the Ten Commandments written on the tables, they testify against sin and rebellion. That testimony must be righteously silenced before anyone can approach God. The so-called ceremonial law could not be called "the *handwriting of ordinances* that was *against us.*" Removal of 'the ceremonial law' is not the ground of forgiveness and acceptance with God. This passage's context is salvation through the atonement of Christ. It is not discussing freedom from the 'ceremonial laws.' If this passage is reduced to refer to merely ceremonial laws, then our blessed Lord shed his blood just so his people could eat bacon with eggs and be free from all the Jewish ceremonial feasts. That would be a distorted view of both the atonement and the great gospel liberty that it purchased.

Paul refers to a list of sabbaths that is knowable. He is talking about 'sabbath days' that can be identified by a clear reference point. Paul expected his readers to know exactly what he meant by 'sabbath.' To my knowledge, Leviticus 23 is the only place in all of Scripture that presents a complete list of 'God's sabbaths.' We will let the Word of God itself tell us what Paul refers to by the words 'the sabbath days' in Colossians 2:15.

> *And the LORD spake unto Moses, saying, Speak unto the children of Israel, and say unto them, Concerning the **feasts** of the LORD, which ye shall proclaim to be **holy convocations,** even these are my **feasts.** (Lev. 23:1, 2)*

God is about to give Moses a list of the ceremonial feasts that are to be observed by Israel. It will include Passover, Feasts of First Fruits, Feasts of Weeks, etc. These feasts are to be 'holy convocations.' Notice carefully the next verse. It establishes clearly what Colossians 2:16 means by 'sabbath days':

> *Six days shall work be done: but the **seventh day** is the **sabbath of rest**, an **holy** convocation; ye shall do **no work** therein: it is **the sabbath** of the LORD in all **your dwellings**.* (Lev. 23:3)

Question: What is the very first *feast,* or *holy convocation,* on the list of ceremonial sabbaths? Answer: *The seventh-day sabbath set forth in the Fourth Commandment!*

The seventh-day sabbath is first on the list of ceremonial sabbaths! It is at the head of the list of the 'feasts, or holy convocations' and cannot be arbitrarily pulled out and separated from the other sabbaths on the list. The Holy Spirit then lists the rest of the holy sabbaths. If you read the entire list of ceremonial sabbaths in Leviticus 23, you will discover that *every* holy sabbath incorporated all of the specific requirements of the seventh-day sabbath simply because they were *all the same in nature.* The Passover, Day of Atonement, etc. did not necessarily fall on a seventh-day sabbath, but they were treated as if they did. If God himself puts the seventh-day sabbath at the head of the only complete list of holy ceremonial sabbaths in Scripture, how dare anyone say that it does not belong there?

Several other factors are significant in verse 3. First, God repeats and reinforces the fact that the essence of keeping the sabbath commandment is to spend the entire day in *rest* and to do *no work:* "the *seventh* day is a sabbath of *rest.*" Secondly, the sabbath was to be observed "in all your *dwellings.*" The sabbath was in no way connected with congregational worship in the tabernacle.

Perhaps it would be a good idea to look at a few passages that demonstrate the importance of a covenant's sign. It will help us to understand the apparent 'out of proportion' punishment in several instances.

Was the incident in Numbers 15:32-36 that serious an offence?

For a long time, I pondered the awful severity of God's judgment on a man for merely picking up some sticks. It was not until I understood the concepts under discussion in this book that I realized what a horrible sin the man had committed. Here is the passage:

> ...*and while the children of Israel were in the wilderness, they found a man that* **gathered sticks upon the sabbath** *day. And they that found him gathering sticks brought him unto Moses and Aaron, and unto all the congregation. And they put him in ward, because it was not declared what should be done to him. And the LORD said unto Moses, The man shall be surely* **put to death:** *all the congregation shall stone him with stones without the camp. And all the congregation brought him without the camp, and* **stoned him with stones, and he died;** *as the LORD commanded Moses.* (Num. 15:32-36)

This was not a case of God being tough on the first offender as an example to others. Picking up sticks on the sabbath was one of the worst possible sins that a man could commit under the Old Covenant. He was breaking the **sign** of the covenant and thereby disavowing the whole covenant. The sabbath was to Israel's relationship with God exactly what a wedding ring is to a marriage relationship. They are both visible signs of a covenant. The ring is given during the ceremony as a sign of the obligation to keep the covenant vows just made. For one partner to take off the ring, throw it at the other person, and walk away would be to deny the entire marriage relationship. This is exactly what sabbath-breaking was under the Old Covenant, since it was the sign of that covenant. Breaking the sabbath renounced the whole covenant relationship with God. To profane the Sabbath by performing even the slightest physical work was to deny all of the vows taken at Mount Sinai. It was an action equivalent to a man deliberately spitting in God's face and then, in defiant self-sufficiency and rebellion, breaking the most important law of the covenant by walking away and picking up some sticks or doing some other physical work.

What is the significance of Exodus 4:24-26?

This incident is another example of the importance of a covenant sign. This extremely instructive event shows how carefully God regards the covenants that he is pleased to make with us.

Moses must have explained a good deal of God's revelation to his wife Zipporah in order for her to do what she did. It is surprising that Moses did not see his inconsistency before his wife saw it. Here is the passage:

> *And it came to pass by the way in the inn, that the LORD met him, and sought to kill him. Then Zipporah took a sharp stone, and cut off the foreskin of her son, and cast it at his feet, and said, Surely a bloody husband art thou to me. So he let him go: then she said, A bloody husband thou art, because of the circumcision.* (Exod. 4:24-26)

God's covenant with Abraham was the basis of the forthcoming deliverance of the children of Israel from Egypt. The sign of that covenant with Abraham was circumcision. Genesis 17:9, 10 makes it clear that circumcision stood for the whole covenant. Verse 11 calls circumcision the sign of the covenant and verse 14 states that an uncircumcised person was to be killed because he had "broken my covenant." Moses' failure to have his son circumcised was, in effect, a repudiation of the very covenant that God was using him to honor. God viewed the action, or rather the inaction, of Moses as an insult worthy of death. Again, we see that failure to honor the covenant sign, even though it is ceremonial in nature, is to despise and reject the whole covenant. It is interesting that Genesis 17:14 specifically states that the uncircumcised person would be cut off from among the people; but in Exodus 4:24 God is about to kill Moses, not his uncircumcised son. Moses was acting as a public person and as God's representative while deliberately disobeying God's covenant sign. Moses was doubly guilty.

We should also mention that Paul told the Corinthians that "many are weak and sick among you, and many sleep" because they misused the Lord's Table, which is the remembrance sign of the New Covenant. The principle of a covenant sign that stands for the whole covenant is not just true for Abraham and Moses; it is true of the New Covenant also. The Lord's Table does not have the place it should have in the life of the church today, and we are suffering the consequences.

A comparison of the Mosaic covenant with other covenants shows that the seventh-day sabbath was the sign of the Mosaic covenant.

When we compare the language used in the Bible to recount the establishment of several covenants, we find that the Ten Commandments were the foundational document of a distinct and separate covenant. The texts also establish that the sabbath was the sign of the covenant given to Israel at Sinai. Look at the following comparisons:

1. The Noahic covenant: *"this is the **sign of the covenant** I have established..."* (Gen. 9:17 NIV).

2. The Abrahamic covenant: *"This is my **covenant** ... you are to undergo circumcision, and it will be a **sign of the covenant** between me and you"* (Gen. 17:11 NIV).

3. The Mosaic covenant: *"... you must observe my Sabbaths. This will be a **sign** between me and you for the generations to come ...The Israelites are to observe the **Sabbath** for the generations to come as a lasting **covenant**"* (Exod. 31:13, 16 NIV).

God made a separate covenant with Moses just as he made a separate covenant with Abraham. The sabbath was the ceremonial sign of the covenant that was written on the tables of stone just as circumcision was the ceremonial sign of the covenant God made with Abraham.

A comparison of the two different reasons for keeping the sabbath day holy helps us to understand the purpose of the 'sign' of the covenant.

The phrase "as the Lord thy God commanded thee" following the commandment to keep the seventh day holy is found in Deuteronomy 5:12, but not in Exodus 20:8. It is obvious why it is not the other way around. The phrase in Deuteronomy 5:12 cannot possibly refer back to Creation because Adam was never "delivered from bondage in Egypt." It has to refer back to Exodus 20:8, since God gave this commandment to Israel at Sinai *after* their deliverance from Egypt. God did not command Adam to keep the sabbath; but he did, at Mount Sinai, command Israel to keep the sabbath as the sign of the covenant that he had just made with them.

Another reason that it is impossible to make the statement 'as the Lord thy God commanded thee' in Deuteronomy 5:12 refer back to Genesis is the specific reason this particular version of the Ten Commandments gives for keeping the sabbath. Deuteronomy 5:15 does not even mention God resting at Creation. It specifically gives the redemption from Egypt as the reason that Israel was to remember the sabbath. How could God possibly have given a commandment in the Garden of Eden to remember Israel's deliverance from Egypt? Imagine either Adam or Abraham being commanded to 'Remember the sabbath day because I delivered you from bondage in Egypt.' It would not have made any sense at all to them.

What do we 'remember' at the Lord's Table?

What is the emphasis in the words our Lord gave us when he instituted the remembrance sign and service of the New Covenant? What should we think when we read or hear the following words?

> *In the same way, after supper he took the cup, saying, "This cup is the **new covenant** in my blood; do this, whenever you drink it, in **remembrance of me."** For whenever you eat this bread and drink this cup, you **proclaim the Lord's death** until he comes.* (1 Cor. 11:25-26 NIV)

What should we feel in our hearts as we take the cup and remember our Lord's words, "This is the New Covenant in my blood"? We should realize that we are celebrating the clear fulfillment of the Old Testament promise concerning the New Covenant. We are remembering the truth symbolized in the emblems (bread and wine), which is that the promised New Covenant is now in full force. Nowhere does the Word of God suggest we are celebrating a new *administration* of the same Old Covenant under which Israel lived. We should have a different feeling than Israel had when God spoke that first covenant from the mountain. Our hearts should feel the liberty and joy of assurance of forgiveness. Feelings of either bondage or fear have no rightful place in our hearts as we rejoice in the memory of the death of our Lord Jesus Christ for our sins. When we remember his promise to come again, hope and joy should fill our minds and hearts.

Would we have a different response if we were Seventh-day Adventists and remembered our reason for worshipping on Sabbath (Saturday) instead of the Lord's Day? We would think of God our creator and lawgiver and the law covenant written on the tablets of the covenant. Our meeting on Saturday (Sabbath) would honor the sign of the covenant under which we were worshipping. We would remind ourselves of the just covenant claims that God makes upon us. The tablets of stone would still be the written code against us because of our sin. As our minds went back to the Old Covenant (Ten Commandments), we would smell the smoke from Sinai and hear its terrible thunder and roar. This would all be reasonable, however, because this is the *exact experience* that Sinai was *supposed to produce* in the consciences of those who were under it as a covenant! This was the stated purpose for which God gave that law in the first place. The purpose of the sabbath sign was to be a reminder of those covenant terms and our duty to obey them. Nowhere does Scripture record any change in the purpose and function of either the covenant or its sign.

The God-designed function of the tables of covenant, or Ten Commandments, was conviction and fear, not joy and hope. The same rules that furnish our *minds* with help in pleasing our heavenly Father functioned in the *conscience* of an Israelite as the condemning *covenant of life and death* (2 Cor. 3:6-18) of their covenant God. However, we must remember that this was God's declared intention in giving the tablets of stone in the first place. Perhaps a chart comparing the remembrance signs and services of the old and new covenants will help make clear what we are saying:

Old Covenant	New Covenant
Points to Creation	Points to Calvary (God's new creation)
Emphasizes Lawgiver and Judge	Emphasizes Christ as Redeemer
"This (keep sabbath) do...	"THIS (remember my death) do...
in remembrance" of your duty	in remembrance of ME."

Christ makes a deliberate contrast when he institutes the remembrance service of the New Covenant. He clearly shows the difference between remembering and celebrating the Old Covenant as compared to celebrating the New Covenant. When Jesus said 'THIS do in remembrance of ME', he was contrasting the New Covenant, and its remembrance sign, with the Old Covenant and its remembrance sign. He was saying, "Instead of keeping the sabbath in remembrance of the old creation and Israel's redemption, THIS do in remembrance of me and the deliverance I have accomplished at Calvary." In other words, remember and think about what the new creation is and how Christ brought it about.

The Old Covenant justly bound men to obey God, upon pain of death, as their creator and lawgiver and celebrated the work of the old creation. The New Covenant binds us to God as our redeemer through our Lord Jesus Christ and celebrates the work of the new creation.[19] One reminds of sin and the other reminds of forgiveness. Read 1 Corinthians 11:25-27, emphasize the word 'this', and think of the contrast that Christ makes between the Old Covenant that he replaced and the New Covenant that he established.

---

[19] The motif of "finishing the work my Father gave" followed by a "resting upon its completion" is a neglected theme. I have developed it in *The Believer's Sabbath,* available from New Covenant Media, 5317 Wye Creek Drive, Frederick, MD 21703-6938.

The sabbath forced Israel to think about two things every week. First, the sabbath-rest reminded them of an Eden they had lost because of sin and rebellion. Their life of sweat and tears was a constant reminder of the life of ease and joy they had lost because of their fall in Adam. Secondly, the sabbath was a constant reminder of the promise that one was coming who would establish a greater sabbath-rest that could not be destroyed by anything. The sabbath was a constant reminder of both the burden of sin and the hope of salvation.

Summary

In this chapter, we have emphasized the importance of covenant signs. The primary importance of the sabbath commandment lies in the fact that it was the sign of the Mosaic covenant God made with Israel at Sinai. The importance of a covenant sign is that it stands for the entire covenant. As I mentioned earlier, the sabbath, as the sign of the Old Covenant, was to Israel what my wedding ring is to my marriage. If I took off my wedding ring, threw it at my wife, and walked out the door, I would by that one act, disavow every oath and promise I made to her. I would repudiate our whole covenant relationship. That is exactly what the man did who picked up sticks on the sabbath. The only way to violate the Fourth Commandment was to do physical work on the sabbath (Exodus 31:12-18); by doing so, the violator threw the wedding ring in God's face.

Moses did the same thing by his refusal to have his son wear the covenant sign of circumcision. Circumcision stood for the whole Abrahamic covenant (Genesis 17:9-14). The only way to violate the Abrahamic covenant was to be uncircumcised. This is why God was so angry with Moses in Exodus 4:24-26. His refusal to wear the wedding ring jeopardized the entire covenant relationship. To violate the sign is to repudiate the whole covenant.

Chapter Eight

The Tablets of Stone Were the Center of Israel's Worship

Everything in Israel's life and worship revolved around the tabernacle. The visible proof that God was among the nation was the cloud by day and the pillar of fire by night. God dwelt behind the veil in the Most Holy Place. There was physical evidence of his presence. That little tent was the most important and holy spot on earth because God's immediate presence was there. Only the High Priest, on the yearly Day of Atonement, was allowed into God's presence in the Most Holy Place. Aaron's most important function of the entire year was to take the blood that had been shed on the altar and sprinkle it on the mercy seat, or lid of the ark of the covenant. As the Most Holy Place was the most holy spot on earth, so the ark of the covenant was the single most holy piece of furniture in that spot. That box was important and holy because of its contents. It contained the covenant document that established Israel as God's special nation. If we understand the purpose and function of the tabernacle and its ministry around the ark of the covenant, we will also understand the nature, function, and purpose of the Ten Commandments. The two serve identical purposes, and the Bible never records that purpose as having changed. Indeed the function did not change—it ended because it was fulfilled! The purpose and function of the tablets of the covenant never changed from the day of their inception at Mount Sinai until the day that written code was nailed to the Cross.

The 'ark of the covenant' was so named because of its CONTENT.

We will review one point covered earlier concerning the ark. The ark of the covenant was built for the express purpose of housing the specific covenant document that established Israel as a nation; that *covenant document was the Ten Commandments.* The ark of the covenant housed the Ten Commandments. It was called the ark of the covenant and the ark of testimony because it held the written covenant that testified against Israel when they disobeyed the covenant terms, or Ten Commandments. All of this is so clear and so simple when we use the terms and phrases used by the Holy Spirit. However, it is very confusing when we start saying the Bible really means "one covenant with two admini-strations" when it speaks of a new covenant that replaces an old and different covenant.

Notice how the following texts establish the contents of the ark:

> *And they shall make an ark of shittim wood: two cubits and a half shall be the length thereof, and a cubit and a half the breadth thereof, and a cubit and a half the height thereof.* (Exod. 25:10)

> *And thou shalt put into the ark the **testimony** which I shall give thee.* (Exod. 25:16)

> *And he spread abroad the tent over the tabernacle, and put the covering of the tent above upon it; as the LORD commanded Moses. And he took and put the **testimony** [the "testimony" is the Ten Commandments] **into the ark,** and set the staves on the ark, and put the mercy seat above upon the ark.* (Exod. 40:19, 20)

The words 'covenant', or 'Ten Commandments', could be in-terchanged with the term 'testimony' in this verse. The ark of the *testimony* is the ark of the covenant. It is clear in the following passages that the 'testimony' in the ark is the Ten Command-ments written on the tablets of stone:

> *At that time the LORD said unto me, Hew thee **two tables of stone** like unto the first, and come up unto me into the mount, and make thee an **ark of wood.** And I will write on the tables the **words that were in the first tables** which thou brakest, and thou shalt put them **in the ark.** And I made an ark of shittim wood, and hewed two ta-bles of stone like unto the first, and went up into the mount, having the two tables in mine hand. And he **wrote on the tables, according to the first writing, the ten commandments,** which the LORD spake unto you in the mount out of the midst of the fire in the day of the assembly: and the LORD gave them unto me. And I turned myself and came down from the mount, and **put the tables in the ark** which I had made; and there they be, as the LORD commanded me.* (Deut. 10:1-5)

Why were the Ten Commandments placed in the ark of the covenant? Why was that box so sacred that human hands were not allowed even to *touch it?* If we want to see how holy the ark was, we only need read 2 Samuel, chapters 5 and 6. When we understand why God instantly killed a man for merely putting his hand on the ark to steady it, we will see the nature, purpose and function of the Ten Commandments that were inside the ark of the covenant. There could be no entrance into the presence of God in the Most Holy Place as long as the tablets of stone in the ark of the covenant were in *force as a covenant document.*

The nature, purpose, and function of the ark of the covenant is the same as the nature, purpose, and function of the Ten Commandments! The Ten Commandments began their ministry of covenant law in the history of redemption when Moses placed them in the box that was designed especially to be their home. Exactly what was the purpose and function of the ark of the covenant and its contents? What particular function did it play in the life and worship of the nation of Israel?

The ark of the covenant prohibited all approach into the immediate presence of God until the terms of the covenant spelled out on the tablets of the covenant had been fully met. Those terms demanded a kind of life that no sinner could produce. Failure to obey the covenant terms written on that covenant document closed off the entrance into God's presence. Aaron alone was allowed, one day a year, to enter the Most Holy Place. He always had to take with him some blood that had been shed on the altar of sacrifice. The purpose and function of the Ten Commandments in the ark of the covenant can be summed up in one word–DEATH. The message in the box was the same message on the veil. You could have put big letters on both the veil and the ark that said: "KEEP AWAY–DO NOT EVEN TOUCH–YOU WILL DIE!" Disobedience to this message caused Uzzah to die (2 Sam. 6:6, 7) and the two sons of Aaron to also die (Lev. 10:1).

Paul presents the same truth in the following passages:

*He has made us competent as ministers of a **new covenant**—not of the letter but of the Spirit; for the letter kills, but the Spirit gives life. Now if the **ministry that brought death, which was engraved in letters on stone.**...* (2 Cor. 3:6, 7 NIV)

*Once I was alive apart from law; but when the commandment came, sin sprang to life and **I died.** I found that the very commandment that was **intended to bring life** actually brought **death.** For sin, seizing the opportunity afforded by the commandment, deceived me, and through the **commandment put me to death.** (Rom. 7:9, 10 NIV)*

Paul saw that the "commandment was ordained to *life.*" However, because of sin, he discovered the commandment was 'death to him.' The tables of the covenant did indeed promise life to anyone that perfectly kept the terms: the Ten Commandments written on the tablets. The same tables also promised death to all who failed to keep those commandments. When Paul specifically says, "...the *very commandment* that was *intended to bring life...,*" he is talking about the tablets of the covenant, or Ten Commandments. If the Ten Commandments, considered as a covenant document, were not a legal/works covenant that promised life for obedience and death for disobedience, then Paul's statements do not make sense.

Jesus responded to the rich young ruler as he did because the Ten Commandments, as a covenant, offered life to those who perfectly obey. The young man wanted to 'earn' his way to eternal life by 'doing', and Jesus told him to 'keep the law' (Matt. 19:17). When the young man asked, "Which one?" Jesus quoted five of the commandments written on the tablets of the covenant and then added the 'second greatest commandment of all' (Lev. 19:18). It is self-contradictory to ask, "If a son of Adam perfectly kept the Ten Commandments, would he not still have his original sin?" The question involves an oxymoron. If the person perfectly kept the law it would prove that he *did not have original sin in the first place.* It is impossible for *any* son of Adam to perfectly obey the law and earn the life it promised simply because *every* son of Adam *has a sinful nature* inherited from his father Adam that keeps him from perfect obedience. The fact that all men have a sinful nature absolutely precludes the first situation, that of a son of Adam perfectly obeying the Ten Commandments, from ever being a possibility. No sinner can earn righteousness by obeying the tablets of stone simply because no sinner can obey them.

However, the tablets of the covenant still *offer life and righteousness* just as surely as they *threaten death and damnation.* The problem that prevents anyone from earning righteousness by keeping the Old Covenant is in the nature of the sinner and not in the nature of the covenant. Our Lord perfectly kept that covenant and earned the righteousness that it promised. As long as the covenant in the ark of the covenant was in force, it closed off any approach to God. It said, 'Stay Away!' No one could meet the terms of that covenant. The 'words of the covenant,' or Ten Commandments, clearly demanded perfect obedience. No one could give the perfect obedience that the covenant justly demanded and thereby earn the righteousness that it promised. Once the covenant had been broken, an acceptable sacrifice had to be offered to take away its curse. The sinner could no more bring an acceptable sacrifice than he could bring a sinless life.

The ministry of the priesthood revolved around the sins against that covenant document in the ark. The blood sprinkled on the mercy seat in the Most Holy Place made the Israelite *ceremonially* clean for *one year* but it could not 'cleanse the conscience' (Heb. 9:15; 10:2, 22). Aaron could present neither a holy sinless life of his own to the covenant nor a blood sacrifice that was sufficient to truly atone and deliver from the curse of the broken covenant. The purpose and function of Aaron's ministry was a constant reminder of sin against the covenant document in the ark of the covenant. Everything was designed to remind people of their guilt. Those in whom the covenant wrought true repentance were given hope in a coming deliverer. However, even they had to live their day-by-day life under the threat of the Old Covenant.

The Lord Jesus Christ, our surety of the covenant, was born under the very law covenant housed in the ark of the covenant. He fulfilled every one of its demands and earned the righteousness that it promised. He then died under the curse of that law covenant (Gal. 3:13), thus forever removing its curse from his people. His endurance of that covenant's curse unto death established the New Covenant, and, through fulfillment, annulled the Old Covenant (the Ten Commandments), and everything that attended it. The proof of this was that God rent the veil from top to bottom. The sign that said 'Stay Out' was changed to 'Enter Boldly.' This change was possible because the terms of the Old Covenant had been fully met. The tables of stone, as a covenant document, were finished and the New Covenant was established forever in the blood and righteousness of Christ.

The priesthood, services, and sacrifices were all necessitated by the terms of the Covenant document in the box. Everything began and ended together.

It is difficult to understand the biblical teaching on the change of covenants that is so clearly set forth in the book of Hebrews unless we see the connection between the ministry of the priesthood and the tables of stone. This is the message of Hebrews chapters 8-10. Notice this section:

> *Now the **first covenant** had regulations for worship* [Do not confuse the actual covenant document, the Ten Commandments, with all of the 'regulations'] *and also an earthly sanctuary. A tabernacle was set up. In its first room were the lamp stand, the table and the consecrated bread; this was called the Holy Place. Behind the second curtain was a room called the Most Holy Place, which had the golden altar of incense and the gold-covered **ark of the covenant.** This ark contained the gold jar of manna, Aaron's staff that had budded, and the **stone tables** of the **covenant*** [Remember, those tablets had the Ten Commandments written on them]. (Heb. 9:1-4)

The purpose for the existence of the priesthood and sacrificial system was to administer the Old Covenant:

> *For this reason Christ is the mediator of a new covenant, that those who are called may receive the promised eternal inheri-*

tance—now that he has died as a ransom to set them free from the sins committed under the first covenant. (Heb. 9:15)

Everything that pertained to Israel's special national relationship to God, including the tablets of the covenant (Ten Commandments), ended when Christ, by his obedient life and death, met every claim and demand of the Old Covenant. Deliverance from the just claims of that covenant was necessary before the true Israel of God could be created and established under the New Covenant. In order to set those under the law 'free from the sins committed under the first covenant', Christ, acting as a surety, had to be 'born under the law' covenant in which he was acting as a surety (Gal. 4:1-7). The tables of the covenant under which he lived and died are now as obsolete as both the ark that housed them and the priestly ministry that sprinkled animal blood on the lid of that ark.

The relationship of the law covenant (the stone tablets in the ark) to the mercy seat (the lid of the ark) is one of the clearest pictures of the gospel in the Old Testament Scriptures. It also sets forth the biblical relationship of law and grace. The tablets of the covenant (Ten Commandments) in the ark represent the just demands of the law covenant. *There you see the 'just, holy, and good law' of God.* The lid of the ark covers the broken covenant of law inside the ark with the blood of atonement. *There you see the free gospel of sovereign grace.* There is not an ounce of grace or gospel in the law covenant document in the box. It is pure law, demanding perfect obedience as the condition of blessing and death as the consequence of disobedience. The blood on the mercy seat covers and hides the broken covenant and the sins against that covenant. That is pure grace!

It was indeed very gracious of God to give the law covenant to convict of sin, and it was even more gracious to provide a payment to cover the sin. But there was no grace in the terms of the covenant document in the box. John Newton had it right: "It was grace (using the law in the box) that taught my heart to fear; and grace (through the blood on the mercy seat) my fears *relieved.*"

Many people want to go straight to the grace part without ever experiencing the fear part. Others seem to have a morbid desire to stay under the fear part and never arrive at heartfelt gospel relief from fear. Newton saw both and in the right order.

Some theologians will challenge the truth that the Ten Commandments offered life and righteousness for perfect obedience. Their theology forces them to deny this biblical fact because it simply cannot acknowledge the validity of any kind of a covenant of *works* after Genesis 3:15. My response to such a view is this: If the tables of the covenant, or Ten Commandments, are not a legal/works covenant document that can award life and righteousness then *we as believers have no righteousness.* Our righteousness is an *earned* righteousness. Christ must have kept some law covenant that had the authority to award obedience with life and righteousness, and thereby earned what it promised. What other law covenant, besides the legal covenant at Sinai, could Christ have possibly been born under to earn this righteousness for us? Did our surety of the covenant endure the curse of a covenant of grace or a legal covenant of works when he died on the Cross? Let each reader find the answers to these questions in his own theological system if he can.

Some writers try to force passages like Galatians 3:24, 25 and Colossians 2:14 to teach that Christ's blood atonement delivered us from the bondage and rigors of the 'ceremonial law.' How can anyone believe that the Father would put his Son to death on the Cross just so his people could be allowed eat pork and avoid circumcision? The very idea is ludicrous. Those who hold this view attempt to prove that the law dismissed in Galatians 3:24, 25 is the 'ceremonial' law and cannot possibly be the Ten Commandments.[20] Such a dismissal of the Ten Commandments is not possible according their system of theology. This is an example of a theological system driving the interpretation of a text, rather than allowing the context to inform one's understanding. The law dismissed in Galatians 3:24, 25 is the very same law under which

---

[20] For a defense of this view, see Chantry, *God's Righteous Kingdom,* 108.

our Lord was cursed in Galatians 3:13. If Galatians 3:10-13 does not teach that Jesus died under the curse of the ceremonial law, why would Paul, a few verses later—Galatians 3:24, 25—be saying exactly the opposite? Is Paul teaching that the curse for not continuing to do everything written in the book of the law only pertains to ceremonies? When Paul writes, "It is written: 'Cursed is everyone who does not continue to do everything written in the Book of the Law'", he is quoting Deuteronomy 27:26. The curses presented in Deuteronomy 27:15-26 include a wide variety of infractions, none of which are ceremonial in nature. There is no indication anywhere in the entire third chapter of Galatians that Paul is limiting his use of the term law to that portion only that pertains to ceremonies. In fact, his use of Deuteronomy 27:15-26 indicates just the opposite; he is using the term in a much more comprehensive sense.

The believer under the New Covenant has constant and immediate access into the presence of God (Heb. 10:17-23) because passages like Galatians 3:24, 25 and Colossians 2:14 *do* refer to the whole Old Covenant—including the tables of stone. The law covenant has been dismissed as the Pedagogue over the conscience of God's people. Regardless of his calling, every saint under the New Covenant enjoys a privilege that even godly Aaron could not enjoy. The function of the tables of the covenant (Ten Commandments) *inside the ark* is just as finished as the ark that held them. They are both finished. The 'doing and dying' of our substitute has removed the yoke on the conscience that kept sinners from entering God's presence. We must neither allow anyone to re-establish that yoke, nor permit anyone to re-hang the veil. We must see the law dismissed forever *as a covenant*. Its sword was wiped clean in our substitute's blood and was forever sheathed that day at Calvary.

Paul's appeal to the Galatians should be tattooed on our minds and hearts:

> *It is for freedom that Christ has set us free. Stand firm, then, and do not let yourselves be burdened again by a yoke of slavery.* (Gal. 5:1 NIV)

To what yoke does Paul refer? It is clearly a reference to law, but what specific law? The defenders of Covenant Theology in its various forms will say, "Paul is talking about the ceremonial law. That is the law that was dismissed and the yoke from which we are set free. Paul could not possibly be talking about the 'moral law.'" We must ask a few questions of such a view. Of what, precisely, does the ceremonial law consist? Even if Paul is talking about ceremonial law here, how is that defined? Once we have arrived at a working definition of this term, we must ask another question. How can the 'ceremonial law' be such a terrible yoke of bondage? Our Lord lived his entire life under every ceremonial law in the Old Testament Scriptures. Is circumcision and abstinence from 'unclean food' such a terrible burden? The orthodox Jews to this day, as well as the Seventh-day Adventists follow the food laws of the Old Covenant with ease and enjoyment. The yoke to which Paul refers is a yoke that is *impossible to bear;* but many have born the so-called ceremonial law without ever considering it as bondage. As I observe the back-to-nature people in our generation, I notice that they follow many of the 'ceremonial' laws of the Old Covenant almost to the letter and never complain of bondage. Their constant cry is the joy and freedom they have found. And these people do not even profess to be doing this out of love to God.

No, this yoke clearly is connected to the blood atonement of Christ. It has to do with something far more serious than mere ceremonies and kinds of food. John Stott has the best comments that I ever read on this passage of Scripture. The italics are in the original, the emphasis in bold type is mine.

> As the New English Bible puts it, *'Christ set us free, to be free men.'* Our former state is portrayed as a slavery, Jesus Christ as a liberator, conversion as an act of emancipation and the Christian life as a life of freedom. This freedom, as the whole Epistle and this context make plain, is not primarily a freedom **from sin**, but rather

from the law. What Christ has done in liberating us, according to Paul's emphasis here, is not so much to set our *will* free from the bondage of sin as to set our *conscience* free from the **guilt** of sin. The Christian freedom he describes is **freedom of conscience**, freedom from the **tyranny** of the **LAW**, the dreadful struggle to keep the law, with a view to winning the favor of God. It is the freedom of acceptance with God and of access to God through Christ. [21]

In a parallel passage, Acts 15, the Holy Spirit clearly defines this yoke of bondage. It is nothing less than the demand that a sinner must earn his own righteousness. This yoke imposes the tablets of stone on the conscience as the 'accuser and excuser.' To make the Ten Commandments to be the doorkeeper guarding God's throne of grace is a yoke on the conscience that no one can bear. That would be to resurrect the ministry of the ark of the covenant in the tabernacle and to put it into the church. The subject discussed at the Jerusalem Council in Acts 15 was not primarily the rule of life for a Christian, but the requirements for salvation of a sinner. Verses 1, 5, and 11 establish the content of the discussion. Some of the believers who belonged to the party of the Pharisees insisted that the Gentiles must be circumcised and keep the law of Moses, not to be sanctified, but to be *saved!*

In verses 8-11, Peter declares that the hearts of the believing Gentiles have been "purified by faith." They, like the believing Jews, had been saved by faith alone without the law. His conclusion is simple and clear. "…Why tempt ye God, to put a **yoke** upon the neck of the disciples, which neither our fathers nor **we** were **able to bear?**" (Acts 15:10). What yoke is this? Whatever it is, the gospel does not deliver men into its bondage. Paul warns against this yoke in Galatians 5:1. It is the yoke the men in Acts 15:1, 5 were trying to impose on the Gentiles. And exactly what were they trying to impose? They were distinctly saying that a sinner had to obey the law *to be saved!* They were putting the law between the sinner and the Savior. They were making the Mosaic

---

[21] John R Stott, *The Message of Galatians* (1968; reprint, with study guide, Leicester, England: IVP, 1992), 132.

covenant to be part of the gospel. They were adding the law to the gospel of grace. The yoke in Acts 15 cannot be ceremonial law, but has to do with a conscience that strives to find acceptance by works. Later in this same chapter (Acts 15:24-29), the council binds some laws that we would categorize as ceremonial (mixed together with laws that we would call moral in nature, without any distinction between the two) on the Gentiles out of respect to the Jewish conscience.

None of the so-called ceremonial laws was a 'yoke of bondage' in and of themselves. Paul instructs believers to sometimes bear the yoke of food restrictions in order to keep a weak brother from stumbling (Romans 14 and 1 Corinthians 8-10). He acknowledges that the observance of special days is practiced by some believers, and considers the decision to do so a matter of liberty. This contrasts sharply with his admonition in Galatians 5:1 to not be burdened by a yoke of slavery. The yoke about which Paul writes in Galatians 5:1, and Peter in Acts 15:10, is the same yoke the writer of Hebrews addresses in Hebrews 9:15. It is beyond question a yoke that cannot be born by anyone. It is nothing less than the law as a covenant laid on the conscience, which results in men wrongly striving to keep the law in order to gain assurance of salvation. The yoke is the awful realization that we have neither the righteous life that the covenant justly demands nor an acceptable sacrifice to give to God to atone for our guilt. We put this yoke on the conscience whenever we use the Ten Commandment as if they were still in the ark of the covenant and not done away in Christ. In doing this, we allow the written code, or Ten Commandments, to once more 'stand against us' (Col. 2:14), instead of seeing the covenant terms written on the tablets of stone forever fulfilled in Christ. The written code, which can only refer to the tables of stone, stood against those under it because they could not meet its just and holy terms. When our surety met those terms, he canceled the 'written code' on the tablets of the covenant. It can never again be against anyone.

We must never allow a Judaizer to use the law covenant against us. The preaching of the law to the conscience with the threat of life and death is a yoke that only a self-righteous Pharisee can pretend to wear. And who has ever met a joyous and victorious Pharisee? As mentioned earlier, people today who make no claim to salvation observe circumcision and the clean food lists, and they do not feel the least burdened. However, the preaching of the law to the conscience with the threat of life and death is a yoke that no one is able to bear.

If we correctly understand the law, we will realize that it can neither bless nor curse us. It cannot curse us because Christ, in our place, perfectly met all of its claims. It cannot bless us because our surety has already earned every blessing it promised. The child of God in Christ is beyond the reach of the law in every sense. I repeat; the law can neither bless us nor curse us. It is not that we are altogether without any law; we are under a higher and more spiritual law—the law of our Lord and Savior.

I could not possibly close this chapter any better than with John Bunyan's classic statement on law and grace. Bunyan taught me the truth that the believer's conscience is set free from the law. The emphasis is mine.

> Therefore whenever thou who believest in Jesus, dost hear the law in its thundering and lightening fits, as if it would burn up heaven and earth; then say thou, I **am freed from this law,** these thunderings have nothing to do with my soul; nay even this law, while it thus thunders and roareth, it doth allow and approve of my righteousness. I know that Hagar would sometimes be domineering and high, even in Sarah's house and against her; but this she must not be suffered to do, nay though Sarah herself be barren; wherefore serve it [the law] also as Sarah served her, and **expel her from thy house.** My meaning is this, when this law with its thundering threatenings doth attempt to lay hold on thy **conscience,** shut it out with a **promise of grace;** cry, the inn is took up already, the Lord Jesus is here entertained, and there is **no room for the law.** Indeed if it will be content with being my informer, and so lovingly leave off to **judge** me; I will be content, it shall be in my sight, I will also de-

light therein; but otherwise, I being now upright without it, and that too with that righteousness, with which this law speaks well of and approveth; **I may not, will not,** cannot, **dare not,** make it my Saviour and Judge, **nor suffer it to set up its government in my conscience;** for so doing **I fall from grace,** and Christ doth profit me **nothing.**[22]

I have used the above quotation by Bunyan on more than one occasion. The usual cry is, "You misrepresent Bunyan's real views." In no way am I suggesting that Bunyan believed everything I believe about New Covenant Theology. Bunyan, like the rest of us, changed his view as he grew in understanding. However, the above is a lengthy quotation from an article specifically written on the subject of the Christian's relationship to the law. With all the cries of 'misrepresenting,' I have yet to have one person try to explain what Bunyan meant by, **"I may not, will not, cannot, dare not,** make it [the law] my Saviour and Judge, **nor suffer it to set up its government in my conscience;** for so doing **I fall from grace,** and Christ doth profit me **nothing."** You may not like or agree with what Bunyan said, but the above quotation is exactly what he said and exactly what he meant. It is also exactly what I believe on the subject of law and grace. You cannot enshrine both Moses and Christ in the conscience of a believer. Only one tenant can occupy the inn of conscience. Bunyan not only states that fact clearly, he repeats himself to make sure you get his message.

My meaning is this, when this law with its thundering threatenings doth attempt to lay hold on thy **conscience,** shut it out with a **promise of grace;** cry, the inn is took up already, the Lord Jesus is here entertained, and there is **no room for the law.**

---

[22] John Bunyan, *The Law and the Christian,* vol. 2 of *Bunyan's Works* (Grand Rapids. MI: Baker, 1999), 388.

Chapter Nine

The Tablets of Stone, or Ten Commandments, as a Covenant Document, Had a Historical Beginning and a Historical End

The moment we say, "The Ten Commandments are finished" *in any sense whatever,* it is impossible for some people to hear what we are actually saying. Their theological receptors hear us saying, "Away with all law in every sense." It does not matter how often or how loudly we affirm our belief in moral law per se and, specifically, in the enduring moral principles of nine of the Ten Commandments written on the tablets of the covenant. That is not enough for these people. They insist that we acknowledge that the Ten Commandments as *written on the tablets of stone at Mount Sinai* are *'the* eternal, unchanging moral law of God.' It is all or nothing. It is impossible to even discuss the clear biblical reasons we have for rejecting such a theological view. "The Creeds and Fathers have spoken and the matter is closed," is the response.

The amusing thing about the people who have this attitude is that although they insist that the sabbath commandment is binding as a part of the eternal, unchanging moral law of God, they never want to discuss anyone's actual practice in regard to 'keeping the sabbath.' It does not matter what a person does, or does not do on Sunday (except attend church services), just as long as he or she theologically acknowledges that the sabbath commandment is part of the eternal, unchanging moral law of God. I have often asked the proponents of this view the following question: "Exactly what would a person in your congregation have to do before you would discipline him out of the church for breaking the Fourth Commandment?" They equivocate for a while and usually wind up saying, "For not attending church." They usually quote Hebrews 10:26 as a proof text. When they are reminded that such a text has nothing to do with church attendance for an Israelite (Israel did not have Sabbath school at 10:00 a.m. and worship service at 11:00 a.m. in the tabernacle), these people have no response. They have a "clear moral absolute' that does not carry even one specific infraction that warrants church discipline. Even if church discipline is practiced, it stops far short of the death penalty demanded by the Mosaic law for infractions of the Fourth Commandment. If the sabbath law is eternal and unchanging, how is it that the penalty for disobedience to it has changed?

We sometimes call these people 'antinominian sabbatarians.' On the one hand, they vehemently insist on laying the Fourth Commandment on the conscience of every Christian as a moral absolute; on the other hand, they refuse to give the Christian any specific rules of what he may or may not do on the holy sabbath day. This view insists that every Christian decide *for himself* what his *own conscience* will or will not allow him to do on Sunday. In *preaching,* the sabbath is one of God's *unchanging moral laws,* but in actual *practice* it is up to the *Christian liberty of each individual* to decide how he will observe it. We believe this is a bit hypocritical. It may even prove that most of the people who teach this view do not, in their own hearts, really believe the 'good and necessary consequences deduced' from their own system of theology. They certainly do not appear willing to put it in into practice. We are not being honest or consistent if we use the thunder and lightening of Sinai to impose the Fourth Commandment on a Christian's conscience and, in the same breath, tell him to treat that 'absolute commandment' as if it were only a 'relative principle' that can be applied any way any individual sees fit.

When I say that the Ten Commandments are finished, I mean *as a covenant document,* or as the *tables of the covenant.* I am NOT talking about the morality contained in the individual commandments. I am talking about the Ten Commandments considered as a single document, specifically as a covenant document. The moral duties commanded on the tablets of stone did not begin at Sinai, but the use of those duties *as the basis of a covenant* did begin there. The content of nine of those ten rules was known by men, and infractions thereof were punished by God long before God gave them to Israel as covenant terms at Sinai. Men were punished for violations of every specific duty commanded in the Ten Commandments *except the Fourth,* or sabbath, prior to Mount Sinai, and likewise, every commandment *except the Fourth,* is repeated in the New Testament Scriptures.

We may disagree with each other on many things about 'the law' but we cannot deny that the Bible clearly teaches the following things:

1. Some specific 'law' had a *historical beginning* at Sinai.

2. That same 'law' that began at Sinai also had a *historical end* at Calvary.

3. The historical beginning of that 'law' is always associated with the *giving of the tablets of the covenant to Israel at Sinai.*

4. The historical ending of that 'law' is always connected with the *coming of Christ and the establishment of the New Covenant.*

It is possible that I totally misunderstand exactly *what specific law* the Bible is talking about, but is it not possible to deny that the above four facts are clearly talking about *some specific law* in the Bible. I think the Scriptures that have been exegeted thus far in this book make it impossible for that law to be anything other than the Ten Commandments written on the tablets of the covenant and given to Israel at Sinai as the basic covenant foundation of their relationship to God. It cannot possibly refer to the so-called ceremonial law nor can it be talking about the law of conscience. It has to refer to the law covenant at Sinai written on stone. For those who disagree, please show me another 'law' in Scripture that fits the four facts listed above and explain the texts that speak of some law 'beginning' and 'ending.'

The historical beginning of the law covenant recorded on the tablets of stone coincided with the beginning of Israel as a nation, or body politic. In chapter 4, we saw these facts set forth clearly in the texts of Scripture that talk about the Ten Commandments.

There is simply no way to understand the following passages of Scripture if we deny that the law has both a historical beginning and historical ending:

> For **before the law was given,** sin was in the world. But sin is not taken into account **when there is no law.** (Rom. 5:13 NIV)

> The **law was added** so that the trespass might increase. But where sin increased, grace increased all the more. (Rom. 5:20 NIV)

> What, then, was **the purpose of the law?** It was **added** because of transgressions **until** the Seed to whom the promise referred had come. **The law was put into effect** through angels by a mediator. (Gal. 3:19 NIV)

> So the **law was put in charge** to lead us to Christ that we might be justified by faith. Now that faith has come, we are **no longer under the supervision of the law.** (Gal. 3:24, 25 NIV)

We cannot read the words *"before* the law," which in this context cannot possibly refer to anything but Mount Sinai, and then try to say that the law that was given was always there. The words 'before the law' mean *before* the law. Those words mean that 'law,' in whatever sense Paul is using the word in this passage, had a historical beginning at Mount Sinai.

The words "the law was *added"* make no sense if the law was already there. Some law, in some sense, has to, in some way, be added at Sinai, or Paul is writing nonsense. This law that was 'added' at Sinai has reference specifically to 'transgressions.' The ministry of the law that began at Sinai *ended* when Christ came. There has to be both a historical beginning and ending to some law, or Paul is talking in circles. There was a given point in time when this law 'was put in charge' and there was another point in time when those to whom Paul is writing ceased to any longer be 'under the supervision' of that same law.

We all agree that Paul cannot mean that man, at Mount Sinai, first became aware of moral duty and conscious that he was to obey those moral duties. How could we explain the behavior of Joseph as a believer and Abimelech as an unbeliever? How could we understand Paul's argument in Romans 2:14? No, Paul is not talking about the effects of conscience in these passages.

We also agree that Paul is not denying that God, before Sinai, punished behavior that was contrary to the moral duties set forth in the law given at Sinai as a covenant. The flood did not occur because God was in a bad mood that day. That event was the direct consequence of the actions of men and women who were living in a manner that they had every reason to know was displeasing to God. They were living in disobedience to the very laws that were 'given' in written form to Israel at Sinai as covenant terms. Law was codified at Sinai and made the terms of a life and death covenant for the first time.

When Paul writes that with the coming of faith, the law is no longer the supervisor of God's people, he is not saying that after Calvary, God ceased to set forth standards of behavior that were pleasing to him and reflective of his character. Our Lord, through his Spirit-guided apostles, continued to reveal the moral character of God to mankind, and to impress on his followers their responsibility to bear the family likeness to the world around them. Paul is saying, however, that whatever the law was that began at Sinai, it also forever ended at the Cross.

It is obvious to me that Paul, in the verses just quoted, is talking about the Ten Commandments purely in *covenant terms.* This has to be the meaning of the word 'law' in Galatians 3 and 4. Galatians 3:13 and 14 teach that Christ died under the curse of some law and, by his death, delivered those who had lived under that same law from that same curse. That law can only be the tables of stone viewed as a covenant document. The 'law' that came four hundred-thirty years after the promise to Abraham has to be, at least on the surface, different in nature from the promise of the gospel given to Abraham, or there is no conflict for Paul to address. Without the conflict, the question in verse 21 of Galatians 3 would be totally unnecessary. The fact that Paul spends so much time answering the problem with a carefully worded argument proves the reality of a problem. The argument is so carefully stated that Paul builds a key point on the use of the singular 'seed' instead of seeds (3:16). The question in Galatians 3:19, "What then was the purpose of the law" is unnecessary if there is no difference at all between the promise given to Abraham and the law given to Moses. Why explain in such detail the difference between two things that are really the same?

According to Galatians 3:22, the *Scriptures, not the law,* declare that the whole world is a prisoner of sin. This is the same message as Romans 3:9-21. All men, without exception, are guilty before God whether they ever had the written law or not. The Jewish ceremonial law alone could never produce that guilt, and the Gentiles did not have the tables of the covenant, or Ten Commandments, to testify against them. This condemnation must be on the ground of the law of conscience. The words in verse 20 can only refer to the giving of the law to Israel at Mount Sinai. The law, in the form of covenant terms, was given to incite and reveal sin. The Jew was put under the law covenant to convict of sin unto justification and also to act as a custodian until Christ came. The law in Galatians 4:4 is the law covenant under which Jesus was born and under which he died. Galatians 4:24 and 25 remove all doubt as to what Paul means by 'the law' in this context:

> *These things may be taken figuratively, for the women represent* **two covenants.** *One covenant is from* **Mount Sinai** *and bears children who are to be slaves:* **This is Hagar.** *Now Hagar* **stands for Mount Sinai in Arabia** *and corresponds to the present city of Jerusalem, because she is in slavery with her children.* (Gal. 4:24, 25 NIV)

When we see that Paul, in these two verses, is talking about the tables of the covenant on which were written the Ten Commandments, or the basic summary terms of the Old Covenant, it resolves the conflict between the law and the promise, and Paul's statements about the law immediately fit together in perfect harmony. We see that when Paul speaks in negative terms about the law, its weaknesses, or its final demise, he is referring to the law covenant (Ten Commandments) written on the Tablets of Covenant.

When Paul speaks of the law in a good sense and applies it to us today, he is either speaking of 'the law' as (1) special revelation, or the Bible, as in Psalm 19:7 and Psalm 1:1, 2 (see also quotation by John Owen on page 46), or (2) he is speaking of the ethical duties contained in the individual verses which continue after the Ten Commandments, as the covenant document, are finished.

The reader is almost sure to be thinking, "That sounds correct. However, if such an easy answer is so clearly set forth in the Bible, *why do many preachers and theologians miss it?*" We raised that very question in the preface. We wrote, "Each person finds only that for which he looks." In the case being discussed, some people cannot hear what Paul is saying simply because it *will not fit into the theological system that they have imposed on the Bible.* In that system, the Ten Commandments cannot be a distinct and separate covenant made only with Israel. The Ten Commandments written on stone tablets at Mount Sinai simply must be identical in every respect to the so-called 'covenant of works' with Adam in Eden. The Ten Commandments cannot *begin* at Sinai in *any sense whatever* in that particular system. It is absolutely essential as the 'good and necessary consequences deduced' from Covenant Theology that the law did not begin at Sinai, or the whole system is destroyed. I will not take time to cover the other verses quoted. The reader may read the verses and try to fit his view of the Ten Commandments into those clear statements concerning the historical beginning and historical ending of the 'the law' and see if they match.

We saw in chapter 7 that the Ten Commandments, or tablets of stone, considered as the covenant document that was kept in the ark of the covenant in the Most Holy Place, were finished when the veil of the temple was rent from top to bottom (Matt. 27:51). Those tablets were instantly as obsolete as Aaron's priesthood and the sacrifices. Aaron's descendants were immediately out of a job. The High Priest also needed a complete new wardrobe, even down to his underwear. He would never again wear either those beautiful high priestly robes or the special white linen underwear that he wore only on the Day of Atonement.

The following facts form the basis of Paul's understanding of the purpose and function of the Ten Commandments today:

One: A new covenant was ratified in the blood of Christ at the Cross. The Old Covenant terms written on the tablets of the covenant at Sinai have been fulfilled and done away. The claims of the Old Covenant have been met; its curse has been endured and removed; and its blessings have been secured by Christ and bestowed on his church.

Two: A new people or nation was 'born in a day' at Pentecost. The true 'holy nation' of 'kings and priests' (the true Israel of God) came into being (Compare Exod. 19:4-6 and 1 Pet. 2:9-11).

Three: A new approach to God was opened the moment the veil was rent from top to bottom. It was the just and holy demands of the tablets of the covenant in the ark of the covenant that had blocked the way into the presence of God. Now the terms of that covenant written on stone have been fully met and we enter boldly into the Most Holy Place (Heb. 10:1-23) robed in the very righteousness the law in the box demanded.

Four: A new status, adult sons of God, with new privileges was given to the 'grown up' people of God, comprised of both believing Jews and believing Gentiles.

Five: A new Pedagogue took over in the conscience of the New Covenant believer. The tables of stone were, in themselves, the old *Pedagogue* in the conscience of an Israelite. That old Pedagogue has been dismissed (Gal. 3:24, 25) and has been replaced by the indwelling Holy Spirit.

Summary

The law, viewed as a covenant document with its content codified for the first time, has a historical beginning at Sinai and a historical ending with Christ. The law covenant did not in any way annul the covenant made with Abraham that promised that all the nations of the earth would be blessed through his seed. This promise was fulfilled in the New Covenant which began when the veil was rent from top to bottom. It is important to see several things. First, even though the law, as codified covenant terms, has a historical beginning at Sinai, the underlying principles of all those laws, except the sabbath, were already revealed to man through the original creation. Neither knowledge of God and his character nor the reality of known sin began at Sinai. Secondly, even though the law, viewed as a covenant document, ended when Christ established the New Covenant, the unchanging ethical elements that underlie the commandments written on the tables of stone are just as binding on us today as they were on an Israelite.

The beginning and the ending of the law covenant has nothing to do with the source or endurance of the ethical standards that reveal God's unchanging character.

Chapter Ten

The Biblical Significance of the Tables of Stone

I have tried to use biblical terms in this book. At various times, I have deliberately used one of six interchangeable terms, or synonyms, when I wanted to refer to the Ten Commandments. One of the terms that the Holy Spirit has used most frequently in reference to the Ten Commandments is *the tables of stone*. It is one of only two of the synonymous terms used in both the Old Testament and New Testament Scriptures. The only other term used in both Testaments is the phrase *the tables of the covenant*. The Holy Spirit did not choose to use the words *Ten Commandments* in the New Testament Scriptures, but he did use these two synonyms. Both of the synonyms used in the New Testament Scriptures include the word *tables*, which not only takes us back to the covenant document at Sinai, but also emphasizes that we are to think of the Ten Commandments as a unit. It seems significant that both the Old and the New Testament Scriptures employ the word 'covenant' when referring to the Ten Commandments (Deut. 9:9 and Heb. 9:4). It would seem that the Holy Spirit wants us to think *covenant* when he refers to the Ten Commandments.

The great significance of the Ten Commandments in the Bible is that they were the actual covenant document upon which everything pertaining to Israel rested. The importance of the tablets of stone, as well as their unique character, is identical to the importance of the Constitution of the United States (See page 53). Nowhere does the Word of God call, or treat, the tables of stone as the 'unchanging moral law of God.' It always connects them to Mount Sinai when God made them the basis of the covenant with Israel. We saw this clearly in a previous chapter.

Various writers in both the Old Testament and New Testament Scriptures will quote an individual commandment out of the Decalogue (and also out of the rest of the Old Testament Scriptures) and use it to reinforce a duty. Our Lord used Deuteronomy

6:6 and Leviticus 19:18 as the foundation to explain what the two greatest commandments in all of Scripture were. Does that mean that the rest of the laws in those chapters are of the same importance as the two that were quoted?

When the Ten Commandments are considered as a *single unit,* or as the 'tablets of stone', they are always viewed as a *'covenant document.'* The question is never, "Do the Ten Commandments contain laws that reveal the unchanging character of God?" Of course they do. We must also ask, "Do the Ten Commandments contain any laws that govern ceremonies that are pictures of Christ and, as such, display God's character in picture form rather than plain words?" Again, the answer will be yes. We only object when someone insists that the Ten Commandments, *as recorded on the tablets of the covenant at Sinai,* are one hundred percent "unchanging moral law." A picture is fine, but the reality is better. The ceremonies that present Christ in shadows and types must change when the real thing has come. We realize that some people's system of theology forces them to hold to the "unchanging moral law" position; however, that position is still wrong. We gladly acknowledge that the tables of stone *contain* laws that reveal the character of God in plain words, but we also believe: (1) those tablets contain some laws that pertain to ceremonies; and (2) they also contain some laws that pertain to ethical behavior that were raised to a higher level by Christ.[23] When we say *raised,* we do not mean *contradicted.*

We must insist that what determines moral conduct for any individual is the specific covenant under which that individual lives. The church is not under the same covenant that God made with Israel at Sinai. Some duties are stated in exactly the same words under both covenants, but some of those duties are defined differently under either covenant. Christians are commanded to *be holy for I am holy.* Peter, in 1 Peter 1:15, 16, quotes verses from Leviticus 11 and 19 as proof texts for this duty. God com-

---

[23] John G. Reisinger, *But I Say Unto You,...* available from New Covenant Media, 5317 Wye Creek Drive, Frederick, MD 21703-6938.

manded both Israelites and Christians to be holy. However, the Israelite demonstrated his holiness quite differently than a Christian does. 1 Peter 1:15, 16 does not tell a Christian to go back to Leviticus 11 and follow the food laws detailed there in order to live a holy life. The duty to be holy is always in effect. The definition of holiness depends on the covenant under which an individual lives. The Christian acquires his definition of holiness, the specific rules for holy living, from the New Covenant Scriptures. The Israelite acquired his rules for holy living from the whole law of Moses.

Sometimes when I am asked, "Do you believe that the Ten Commandments are the rule of life for a Christian?" I reply, "That depends on what you mean. If you mean (1) the Ten Commandments as they are written on the tablets of stone, then the answer is no. If you mean (2) the Ten Commandments as they are interpreted and applied by our Lord and his apostles in the New Covenant Scriptures, then the answer is yes. They are a vital part of my rule of life."

This is exactly what Paul teaches in Ephesians 2:19, 20. We must take this text of Scripture seriously. These words are the Words of God! If I am wrong in my interpretation of these verses, then all of the following conclusions that I make must be rejected. However, if this passage really means exactly what it says, then we are forced to acknowledge that Israel and the church have two different canons of conduct. Look carefully at the text:

> *Consequently, you are no longer foreigners and aliens, but fellow citizens with God's people and members of God's household, built on the **foundation of the apostles and prophets,** with Christ Jesus himself as the chief cornerstone.* (Eph. 2:19, 20 NIV)

Nearly all commentaries on this text written fifty years ago or earlier will say, "The phrase, 'Apostles and prophets,' means the Old and New Testaments Scriptures." More recently, we find men saying, "The word prophets may refer to the New Testament prophets." Today, most commentators will insist that the word 'prophets' must mean the *New Testament* prophets and cannot possibly mean the Old Testament prophets. William Hendrickson is typical in his commentary:

> The position that the term *prophets* as here used refers to the Old Testament bearers of that appellative, such as Moses, Elijah, Isaiah, Jeremiah, etc., (thus Lenski, *op. cit.,* pp.450-453), is open to serious objections; such as the following: (1) Apostles are mentioned first, then prophets; (2) the designation of 'foundation' of the house, a dwelling shared *equally* by Jew and Gentile, suits the New Testament prophets better than those of the older dispensation; (3) according to 4:8-11 the prophets there mentioned immediately after the apostles, just as here in 2:20, are 'gifts' bestowed on the church by the ascended Christ; hence, prophets of the New Testament era; and (4) 3:5, where the same expression 'apostles and prophets' occurs in a context from which the reference to the prophets of the old dispensation is definitely excluded, would seem to clinch the argument in favor of New Testament prophets.[24]

You, as I, may find it hard to believe that a convinced Covenant Theologian would make such statements. I admire him for being honest with the words and truth of the text, even if what he writes cannot be reconciled with his own theological system. His comments demonstrate beyond question that Paul refers to New Testament apostles and New Testament prophets. John Stott takes Hendriksen's correct exegesis one step further and presents its biblical and theological implications. Both men agree that the term 'prophets' in Ephesians 2:19, 20 refers not to *Old Testament* prophets, but to *New Testament* prophets. Stott not only says that the text refers to New Testament prophets, but he also demonstrates that this clear fact has profound theological implications. The life and worship of the church is not built on Moses, his laws, or the covenant terms that established Israel as a nation. The foundation of the church is Christ himself, and her life and worship is governed through his laws. Christ, the new Lawgiver, gives those laws through the New Covenant apostles and proph-

---

[24] William Hendrickson, *New Testament Commentary, Ephesians* (Grand Rapids: Baker Book House, 1967), 142.

ets in the inspired New Covenant Scriptures. John Stott has said it better than I can. The emphasis is mine.

> The couplet 'Apostles and Prophets' may bring together the Old Testament (prophets) and the New Testament (apostles) as the basis of the church's teaching. But the inverted order of the words (not 'prophets and apostles' but 'apostles and prophets') suggests that probably the New Testament prophets are meant. If so, their bracketing with the apostles as **the church's foundation** is significant. The reference again must be to a small group of inspired teachers, associated with the apostles, who together bore witness to Christ and whose teaching was derived from revelation (3:5) and was foundational.
>
> **In practical terms this means that the church is built on the New Testament Scriptures. They are the church's foundation documents.** And just as a foundation cannot be tampered with once it has been laid and the superstructure is being built upon it, so the New Testament foundation of the church is inviolable and cannot be changed by any additions, subtractions or modifications by teachers who claim to be apostles or prophets today. The church stands or falls by its loyal dependence on the **foundation truths which God revealed to his apostles and prophets, and which are now preserved in the New Testament Scriptures.** [25]

One of the implications of Ephesians 2:20, as John Stott says, is that there is a historical shift of authority from the Old Covenant to the New Covenant. The life and worship of Israel was built on Moses and the laws given to him, including the tables of the covenant, at Sinai. The life and worship of the Body of Christ is built on the New Testament Scriptures given to the church by Christ and his apostles. During Israel's history, many different prophets delivered the specific laws that were necessary to administer the Old Covenant. In the New Testament Scriptures, Christ and his apostles deliver the laws that are necessary to govern a community based on grace. The full and final authority over

---

[25] John R. Stott, *God's New Society, the Message of Ephesians* (Downers Grove, IL: IVP, 1979), 107. For another excellent presentation of this same position, see Loraine Boettner in, *The Meaning of the Millenium: Four Views*, ed. Robert G. Clouse (Downers Grove, IL: IVP, 1977), 95-103.

the church's life and worship is not Moses and the laws of the earthly theocracy. Her full and final authority is the Lord Jesus Christ, the new lawgiver who replaces Moses. He expresses and defines his will and authority through his Word: the New Testament documents inspired by the Holy Spirit. That is precisely what Paul means in Ephesians 2:19, 20. John Stott has clearly understood and set forth the meaning of this text.

I am not suggesting that the Old Testament Scriptures only set forth laws that govern behavior restricted to ceremonies and/or civil action. Nor am I saying that the principles upon which these other laws are based are not meant to govern the moral behavior of all men in all ages. I also agree that the laws that are clearly confined to governing the ceremonies and/or civil activities of a theocracy have been done away in Christ. That is too obvious for anyone to deny.[26] However, that is far different than creating *clear-cut complete lists,* or *specific codes of law,*[27] and (1) designating one list as 'THE moral law', another list as 'THE ceremonial law,' and yet one more as "THE civil law", then (2) keeping one list and throwing away the other two. The Scriptures know nothing of this approach in establishing moral behavior for either a Jew under the Old Covenant or a Christian today under the New Covenant. The only clear-cut list that was written in a codified form was the 'words of the covenant' or Ten Commandments,

---

[26] I am not contradicting what I said earlier. We, today, may refer to a given commandment as 'ceremonial in nature' and therefore no longer binding. However, an Israelite could never have done the same thing. He was just as 'morally' bound to obey a food law as any of the Ten Commandments. We may be able to see the difference between moral, ceremonial, and civil and be able to act accordingly. An Israelite may have recognized that idolatry was different in nature from eating unclean food, but he was not free to act upon that distinction and eat the unclean food. The 'law of Moses' was one ball of wax, a complete package, with no options.

[27] A good friend decided to read the Pentateuch and use three different colored pens to highlight the moral, civil, and ceremonial law. He was soon amazed that it was impossible.

and that 'written code', considered as a covenant document, was 'nailed to the Cross' in Christ (Col. 2:14).

We continue to emphasize that our position is that the Ten Commandments were done away *only when considered as a* **covenant document.** We are *not* saying that the principles expressed in the demands of the individual commandments have ceased. Our Lord Jesus Christ retains the principles that underlie commandments regardless of where those commandments are found in the Old Testament Scriptures. Christ did indeed drop some commandments that governed ceremonies; with the abolition of those ceremonies, laws to govern them were no longer needed. The sabbath commandment is just such an example. Christ also changed some commandments by raising their demands to a much higher level. The Mosaic law of divorce is an illustration of this fact. Christ also added some new laws that are consistent only with grace and inconsistent with the law of Moses. This is why Moses could never have written the Sermon on the Mount.

Wherever Paul's words in Ephesians 2:20 are minimized or ignored, and Moses accorded equal (which actually is *greater)* authority over the worship and conscience of either the church or the individual Christian, there is a clear denial of the unique and final authority of the lordship of Christ over the church.

All that the Old Testament Scriptures predicted and looked forward to concerning the church has been, or is being, accomplished in the person and work of Christ. The new nation, the true dwelling place or temple of God, the true house of God, the priesthood, the new sonship status, and the gift of the Spirit of adoption are all present realities. All of these things are possible only because of the *new foundation* laid in the New Covenant. The lordship of Christ, expressed in his Word by his Spirit in the New Covenant Scriptures, is that which defines and mediates all of the above things, including the New Covenant itself. Until this shift from the old authority of Moses to the new authority of Christ is seen, recognized and clearly articulated, we deny, even if unknowingly, the lordship of Christ as the new lawgiver over the life and worship of the church. We reject the chief corner-stone when we reject the uniqueness and total newness of the new building (Eph. 2:11-22) and act as though no distinctly new building has been built. In essence, we deny that Jesus Christ himself is the new foundation upon which the 'new creation' has been built.

When Israel is treated as exactly analogous with the body of Christ, then Moses must be not only equated with Christ as an equal lawgiver, but Moses must actually be made the greater lawgiver and Christ merely the greatest interpreter of Moses, because Moses came first. When the church, as the body of Christ, is not seen as a radically 'new man' (Eph. 2:15) or part of a completely 'new creation' (2 Cor. 5:17) that was unknown before the day of Pentecost, it will always follow that Christ is rejected as a new lawgiver. Christ becomes merely the obedient disciple, or law *keeper,* of Moses, but he dare not be a law *giver* in his own right. At most, Christ is the final and greatest rabbi. In such a theology, we should call the Sermon on the Mount "The Talmud of Jesus" since he is only an interpreter of Moses and not a lawgiver in his own right.

The key question that we are discussing in this book is this: "What is the great significance of the Ten Commandments, or tablets of stone, in the mind of the writers of Scripture?" Are the tables of the covenant the unchanging moral law of God and therefore the Christian's rule of life? If we answer that question with the Scriptures themselves, our answer will always be, "The Ten Commandments are viewed as the basic terms of the Old Covenant that God made with Israel at Sinai." The Bible never leads us to answer that question by saying, "The tables of the covenant are God's unchanging moral law." Our creeds may force us to respond that way, but the Scriptures will not allow us to do so.

If the discussion shifts from the tablets of the covenant, or Ten Commandments, as a covenant document to any individual or specific duty commanded in the words of the covenant, the questions should change accordingly. We would then be discussing an entirely different subject. The question would have to become, "Are the Ten Commandments, or tablets of stone, *as given at Mount Sinai,* the most complete revelation of the moral character of God ever given, and therefore totally sufficient to be the standard for the Christian's rule of life today?" We should answer, "Absolutely Not!" The tables of the covenant, or Ten Commandments, are not the fullest revelation of God's character that was ever given, and they are certainly not sufficient for the Christian's rule of life as he lives under grace. As I said above, "The Ten Commandments, *as they are interpreted and applied by our Lord and his apostles,* are a vital *part* of a Christian's rule of life." However, that is an entirely different statement from, "The tables of the covenant given to Israel are the rule of life for Christians today."

We do not in any way demean Moses when we insist that the tablets of stone are only a dim shadow when compared to the words of Christ in the Sermon on the Mount, any more than we demean Aaron when we insist that he and his ministry are finished because Christ has replaced Aaron as High Priest. Why would we refuse to send men back to Aaron and his ministry, and then insist on sending them back to Moses and his ministry? Does Christ not equally fulfill both the prophecy concerning a new and greater prophet who would arise to replace Moses (Deut 18:15-19), and the prophecy of the establishment of a priesthood that would replace Aaron's?

When considered individually and independently of its covenant status, each of the commandments written on the tablets of the covenant stands entirely on the interpretation and application of that commandment by Christ and his apostles. Some of the commandments remain in force exactly as they were given at Sinai; some are changed and raised to a higher level; one is dropped, or at least totally spiritualized; and some are redefined and enlarged. I believe that our Lord Jesus Christ has every right to make all of these changes. I love Moses and acknowledge his greatness, but I love Christ more and believe he is far greater. The tablets of stone were indeed the most stringent moral code ever given *up to that point in time,* but the Sermon on the Mount is a much higher and demanding moral code than the tables of stone. The New Covenant Scriptures must interpret the Old Covenant Scriptures; the glossary that defines the meaning of true holiness for a child of God today is found in the back of the Book and not the front.

The Ten Commandments *contain* much unchanging law that governs moral behavior and is just as binding on the church today as it was on an Israelite. However, that position is different from one that equates the tablets of the covenant with a so-called 'eternal moral law.' I reject the adamant insistence of some theologians that the tablets of stone are, in their *entirety* and *as given at Sinai,* the 'highest moral law ever given' and therefore 'totally sufficient, when correctly understood, for the Christian's rule of life today.' Such a theology makes it impossible for these people to accept the clear fact that the Ten Commandments are the distinct covenant document that established Israel's nationhood.

I know this may appear to be a gross over-simplification, but it is not! It is just as clear as the doctrine of justification by faith—if we begin with the Scriptures themselves and let the words and phrases mean exactly what they say. Why do men refuse to deal with the Ten Commandments as a distinct covenant document when the Scripture is so clear? Why do they deny the clear fact that the tablets of stone are a vital part of the actual 'Old Covenant document' that was made with Israel and done away in Christ?

I was attending a conference in New England several years ago where I delivered a message that demonstrated that the primary function of the tablets of stone was to convict of sin and prepare lost sinners for grace. A young man challenged my message and said, "I agree that is *one* function of the law but not the *primary* function." He then proceeded to explain that the Ten

Commandments were given to a redeemed people as a 'custodian' and were meant to protect the gospel and keep the people from wandering into sin and idolatry. When asked if the message I had just preached had used Scripture verses to prove the point, the young man replied, "Yes, but the message did not show from Scripture the *primary purpose* of the law." I responded, "You show me the texts of Scripture that prove the point that you are trying to make and you believe was missed in my sermon." After several long minutes of deep thought, the young man grinned and replied, "Why am I so dogmatic about something for which I do not have a single verse of Scripture?" I then discussed with him some of the foregoing material concerning the status of the tables of stone as a legal covenant document. He finally asked, "Why have I never before thought of the Ten Commandments as *even a covenant document* let alone a *legal* covenant document?" Earlier, the young man had informed me that he had just finished listening to four tapes on the covenants and read several books about the correct relationship between the law and the gospel. It was not possible to resist saying, "The answer to your question may be that you read too many books and listen to too many tapes and do not read enough of the Bible." He again grinned and said, "You may be right."

The concept of 'moral, ceremonial, and civil' codes of law does not grow out of reading the Scriptures. It is a literary device whose use has come to be equated with biblical terminology. The idea of *categories* of law must be replaced with the truth that the *covenant* in force at a given time is the basis for the establishment of morality and holiness for any individual under that covenant. God's commandment to Israel to 'be ye holy, for I am holy' is an identical commandment given to Christians today. When Peter exhorts us to be holy, he quotes from the Old Testament Scriptures (Lev. 11:44-45; 19:2; 20:7, etc.). However, in order to carry out the commandment 'to be holy', given in 1 Peter 1:15, 16, something is required that is very different from the demands of the identical commandment given to Israel under the Old Covenant in Leviticus 11 and 19. Failure to see this difference makes it impossible to see the correct relationship of the laws of the Old Covenant to a believer's life today.

We cannot possibly understand how David could enter into a polygamous marriage with Bathsheba, with God's expressed approval and blessing, without understanding the change in the terms of the 'Be ye holy, for I am holy' commandment when it is given under the New Covenant. David could be holy in God's sight under the Old Covenant and practice polygamy, but a believer today under the New Covenant can not do the same thing.[28] Polygamy did not break the Seventh Commandment (you shall not commit adultery) under the Old Covenant, but it does violate the new and higher moral law that Christ gave the church in the New Covenant (Matt. 19:1-9). Either the definition of adultery has changed under the New Covenant, or David lived his life in a multiple-adulterous situation.

We would all categorize the eating of unclean animals as 'ceremonial' in nature and place it on the 'ceremonial law list' (Lev. 11:44-46). Likewise, we would certainly have to classify respect for our parents (Lev 19:2, 3) as belonging on a 'moral list.' But the Holy Spirit put both laws together on the *same list* under the Old Covenant. This kind of mixing of laws is even more clearly demonstrated in Leviticus 19:18, 19. In these two verses, one of the two greatest 'moral' commandments in all of Scripture ('love your neighbor as yourself') that, according to Christ (Matt. 22:39, 40), undergird *all of man's duty* to God is mixed together with 'ceremonial' laws concerning animal husbandry, agronomy and clothing.

Notice this fact in the following passage:

> *Do not seek revenge or bear a grudge against one of your people, but* **love your neighbor as yourself.** *I am the* LORD. *Keep my*

---

[28] See Reisinger, *But I Say Unto You,* ... for a discussion of the change from the canon of conduct under which Israel lived to the canon of conduct under which the church lives. It is vital that this change of canons be understood, especially as the two different canons relate to the polygamy and easy divorce allowed under the Old Covenant.

*decrees. Do not **mate different kinds of animals.** Do not plant your field with **two kinds of seed.** Do not wear clothing woven of **two kinds of material.*** (Lev. 19:18, 19 NIV)

In this text from Leviticus, the Holy Spirit put the *second highest 'moral' commandment in all of Scripture* right in the middle of what would have to be designated ceremonial laws. Was Jesus conscious of the immediate context when he took a phrase from Leviticus 19:18 and turned it into the second greatest commandment in all of the Word of God? Jesus obviously did not think of the Ten Commandments as the highest moral standard ever given. The text from which Jesus quotes gives no indication that verse 18 is a great 'moral' law and the surrounding laws are only 'ceremonial.' Nor is there the least indication in the text that we are to be prepared to receive a command of supreme importance. Both the first and second 'greatest commandments' are given as almost off-handed statements when placed in their contexts. It is only when Christ chooses to use Leviticus 19:18, as he does in Matthew 22, that the phrase in this text becomes the 'second highest commandment' upon which all other law, including the Ten Commandments, hang. Deuteronomy 6:5 and Leviticus 19:18 are *not* the 'summary' of the Ten Commandments. *It is the other way around!*

Let us look at the context of the 'second highest commandment' in Leviticus 19:

*The LORD said to Moses, "Speak to the entire assembly of Israel and say to them: '**Be holy because I, the LORD your God, am holy.** Each of you must **respect his mother and father,** and you must **observe my Sabbaths.** I am the LORD your God. ..."Do not seek revenge or bear a grudge against one of your people, **but love your neighbor as yourself.** I am the LORD. Keep my decrees. **Do not mate different kinds of animals.** Do not plant your field with **two kinds of seed.** Do not wear clothing woven of **two kinds of material.** ...Do not **eat any meat with the blood** still in it. "'Do not practice **divination or sorcery.** Do not cut the **hair at the sides of your head** or clip off the **edges of your beard.** Do not cut your bodies for the dead or put tattoo marks on yourselves. I am the LORD. Do not de-*

grade your daughter by making her a prostitute, or the land will turn to prostitution and be filled with wickedness. Observe my **Sabbaths** and have reverence for my sanctuary. I am the LORD.'" (Lev. 19:1-3, 18, 19, 26-30 NIV)

Neither our Savior nor Moses, the writer of Leviticus, divided the various laws presented in Leviticus 19 into different kinds of lists. The chapter begins with the identical exhortation of 'Be holy for I am holy' that Peter gives to Christians (1 Pet. 1:15, 16). The above verses, quoted from Leviticus 19, cover honoring parents, keeping the Sabbath, loving our neighbor as ourselves (the 'second greatest law'), and then immediately proceed to prohibit the mixing of different seed and different cloth, and crossbreeding of animals. It is impossible to miss the fact that some of these laws are exceedingly different in their nature. It is just as impossible to try to create two lists of laws, one 'moral' and the other 'ceremonial,' out of these verses. However, when this clear fact is admitted, we must (1) either deny that Leviticus 19:18 is, according to Christ, the second highest 'moral' law in the Bible, or we must (2) admit that it is impossible to create a 'moral' and a 'ceremonial' list of laws in Leviticus 19. Does the passage itself teach that the second highest 'moral' commandment in Scripture ("love your neighbor as yourself," verse 18) is to be put on the same list with the very next verse, which contains instructions on making cloth, breeding livestock, and planting seed (verse 19)? Was the Holy Spirit playing games with us when he wrote Leviticus 19, or was he showing us how utterly futile and wrong it is to think in terms of a 'moral' list and a 'ceremonial' list of laws?

It is amazing that anyone can read Leviticus 19:26, which prohibits eating blood and practicing witchcraft, then read the next verse, 27, which discusses how not to cut your hair and beard, and believe that the Old Covenant laws are divided up into 'civil, ceremonial and moral' lists. *All of the laws* given in Leviticus 19 were equally important and binding on an Israelite. As the Israelite tried to obey God and 'be holy,' he was as duty bound to God to attach the same importance to his diet and haircut as he did to the treatment of his parents, his observance of the sabbath, and his love for his neighbor. Laws that forbid tattoo marks are placed right next to those that prohibit making your daughter a prostitute, without any discernable difference in importance.

In no way could an Israelite living under the law of Leviticus 19 ever discern that 'love your neighbor as yourself' was the 'second greatest "moral" duty' for him to obey. In the text, this law was no more significant than those that instruct him how to plant his fields correctly. The same thing is not even close to true today. There is a very great difference in the respective importance of those same things under the New Covenant. In other words, *how* an Israelite lived in order to obey the commandment 'be ye holy' was different in many respects from how a Christian lives today in obedience to the identical commandment. The duty to 'be holy' is just as essential for a Christian as it was for an Israelite, but how each one fulfills that duty is radically different. The way to ascertain that difference is definitely not by the arbitrary creation of a 'civil law' list, a 'moral law' list and a 'ceremonial law' list.

We are NOT saying that there are no *individual* laws that are 'moral' in their very nature. Leviticus 19:18 is surely such a law. We also believe there are other laws that are 'ceremonial or civil' in nature; the very next verse, Leviticus 19:19, is an example. We are insisting that neither Moses nor Christ, nor anyone else in all of Scripture ever created lists and used the different lists as the foundation of moral versus ceremonial or civil conduct.

Let us summarize what we are saying:

One: There is a radical difference in the specific laws that an Israelite and a Christian follow in order to obey the commandment 'Be ye holy, for I am holy.' Even the shallowest comparison of 1 Peter and Leviticus 19 will show this.

Two: That which makes the difference is NOT discovered by arbitrarily created 'lists' of different kinds of laws. That is simply impossible. None of the writers of Scripture in either the Old or New Testament even hinted at such a method.

Three: Our duty to God is defined by the laws of the specific covenant under which we live. The Old Covenant was accompanied by a series of all kinds of laws given at various times through prophets. All of these were equally part of 'the law of Moses' and therefore equally binding on an Israelite because he was a member of the theocracy. The New Covenant is accompanied by new and higher laws given by Christ and the apostles, and these laws are all binding on a Christian because he is a citizen in the kingdom of Christ. There is no New Covenant theocracy.

Four: The commandment to 'Be ye holy, for I am holy' is identical in both covenants. However, the specific laws to be obeyed in order to be holy are not the same. There are many instances where the duty is identical in both cases, but there are also instances where the duties are radically different.

Five: Anything that is intrinsically 'moral' in its nature is always moral. Even God can not make something moral that is immoral. However, we dare not arbitrarily decide what is moral and what is not. We obey all of God's laws that he tells us to obey, simply because he says so. God may take a law (and he definitely has) that governs a ceremony and make obedience to that particular law a matter of life or death. This is the case with both the sabbath and circumcision when God made them covenant signs. For a Jew to break these 'ceremonial' laws was to commit a grievous 'moral' (?) sin, simply because they were sins against the covenant signs (Exod. 4:24-26 and Num. 15:32-36). Touching a dead body was not intrinsically 'immoral', but it was still a great sin under the Old Covenant. Was eating shrimp 'moral disobedience' for an Israelite? Did God turn an 'immoral act' (?) of eating pork into a 'morally neutral' act when Christ came? These are the kinds of difficult questions that arise when categorical lists are created.

We have not understood the message of the New Testament Scriptures until we see the historical shift from the authority of Moses to the full and final authority of Christ. Christians are not under the authority of Moses as their lawgiver.[29] They are under the authority of Christ, the new lawgiver. Christians are not under the Old Covenant and do not use it to define their moral absolutes any more than they use it to define their diet. They are under the New Covenant, and it defines everything in their life and worship either by clear precept or personal application of a principle. Oftentimes the principle will be a spiritual application of an Old Covenant law. Paul's use of Deuteronomy 25:4 is one example: ... *'Do not muzzle an ox while it is treading out the grain.' Is it about oxen that God is concerned? Surely he says this for us, doesn't he?'* ... (1 Cor. 9:9, 10). This is a clear illustration of how a believer uses the Old Covenant Scriptures. Christians are in no sense lawless. They are under higher laws and a greater obligation to be holy because of Calvary. The difference in their holiness consists in both the specific laws that they obey as well as their motive for doing so. This in no way means that the Old Covenant did not demand heart obedience as well as mere outward conformity. It does mean that grace, in its very nature, can and does, because of the Cross, make higher demands on regenerate people than even the 'holy, just, good' law can ever make.

Perhaps it would be good to illustrate what has just been said. The American colonies were under the constitution and laws of England up until 1776. In that year, the colonies became the United States of America. They united under the Constitution of the United States. From that moment, they were 'under a new rule.' The laws and Constitution of England no longer had any legal authority over any American. The laws of England, as such, were totally nullified in respect to us as a nation. None of England's laws could be appealed to as the final authority on any matter whatsoever. America was under the authority of a new constitutional document or covenant. The Constitution of the United States was now the full and final authority over every

---

[29] See *Christ, Lord and Lawgiver Over the Church*, by John Reisinger (Frederick, MD: New Covenant Media, 1998). Available from New Covenant Media, 5317 Wye Creek Drive, Frederick, MD 21703-6938.

American. That is the exact parallel between the tablets of the covenant given to Israel and the New Covenant given to the church. That which established and governed Israel as a theocracy is no longer in effect over the church.

It is clear that the framers of the United States Constitution carefully considered and used many of the laws of England when they wrote the new laws. However, that is not the point. The significance is in the change from life under the law of England to life under the law of the United States. That constitutes a complete change, regardless of how many laws are new, the same, or different. That is precisely what the Bible means when it compares the legal covenant that governed Israel and the gracious covenant that governs the church.

We simply must stop asking and answering catch questions that are purely theological and not biblical and then using the 'yes' or 'no' simplistic answers as a means of labeling someone either an antinomian or a legalist. It is this form of logical deduction that locks us into a man-made system that has been placed above the Word of God. This approach forces people to divide into antagonistic camps on the basis of how they answer the catch questions.

It is a sin against God and his church to label a Christian as antinomian simply because he believes the sabbath was the ceremonial sign of the law covenant and not an 'eternal, unchanging moral law.' This is doubly true when the accused person affirms and clearly teaches that Jesus reissued the other nine commandments, and thus they are just as morally binding on a Christian as they were on the Jews. At worst, such a person is only one-tenth an antinomian and nine-tenths a 'nomian' or lover of the law.

It is also sinful to label a person a 'legalist' for believing and seeking to obey all ten of the laws just as they are written on the tablets of stone. This is doubly true when that person affirms and teaches that such obedience neither saves him nor keeps him saved. Obedience to what we sincerely believe is the revealed will of God as it is set forth in objective commandments *is not legalism!* It is the proof of a holy heart! Some of the godliest people I know sincerely believe that the sabbath is a moral commandment binding on Christians today. I have the deepest respect for them and would not tolerate any suggestion that they are legalists. I do agree that a failure to understand *which laws* God wants us to keep may lead to a legalistic life style, but it is not at all inevitable. However, the problem in such a case is due to a misunderstanding of the truth of God's Word and not a legalistic heart. This is the very problem that Paul deals with in 1 Corinthians 8-10 and Romans 14. Notice that Paul does not label the weak brother a legalist nor does he label the strong brother an antinomian.

Summary

The biblical significance of the tablets of stone is that they are the covenant document upon which Israel's national status rested. Under the New Covenant, the individual laws contained in that covenant document must stand or fall as Christ decides. Some duties are stated in identical terms under both covenants, but are defined differently under each; some commands are directly transferred from one covenant to another, and some laws are changed. The church's status as a holy nation rests upon the foundation of the atoning work of Christ. He fulfills every type and shadow. The life and worship of the New Covenant people of God is built on the New Covenant Scriptures given through the apostles and prophets. The church is bound to obey the commands given to her by her new lawgiver—Jesus Christ—in the form in which he issues those commands. Let us stop sinning against our brothers by using theological systems to label each other either as antinominians or legalists. Let us instead ask this question: Does my attitude toward my brother fit into Paul's exhortation and benediction to the Galatians?

> *May I never boast except in the cross of our Lord Jesus Christ, through which the world has been crucified to me, and I to the world. Neither circumcision nor uncircumcision means anything; what counts is a new creation. Peace and mercy to all who follow this rule [canon], even to the Israel of God.* (Gal.6:14-16 NIV)

Let us fulfill the revealed will of God to love deeply, from the heart (1 Pet. 1:22), all those who boast in nothing but Jesus Christ and him crucified, and who walk in sincerity under the canon of conduct that clearly reveals the will of God for his redeemed church.

Chapter Eleven

Conclusions

The time has come to insist that discussions of biblical subjects be based on the Bible itself and not on rigid theology and creeds. If our creeds and theology are truly biblical, then all we need to do is examine the Bible verses from which we originally established the tenets we are now defending. If there are texts in the Bible that clearly teach the truths that our fathers put into the creeds, then those verses *are still in the Bible* and they *still teach the same truth.* A sincere Bible teacher should welcome the opportunity to take the Bible and *textually* prove the biblical accuracy of his creed. If he either cannot, or simply will not, attempt to prove his doctrines with the Bible itself, but insists that 'the creeds have already settled all these issues,' then he has clearly revealed his real attitude to both the Word of God and to the creeds. And it is obvious which one is his *final* authority! It may also suggest that the people who formulated the creed in the first place used logic and prejudice at some points when they lacked actual Scripture texts. It is unsettling to contemplate the possibility that what one has believed to be God's will, may not be biblical after all. If one's identity as a Christian is wrapped up in theological and creedal distinctions, then to question those systems and creeds is to call into question one's very perception of himself as a Christian. Perhaps this is one of the reasons some men choose to hide behind creeds today and refuse to discuss the Word of God itself.

When asked if the 'moral law,' meaning the tables of the covenant, is the rule of life for a Christian today, the answer should be, "the entire Word of God is the Christian's rule of life (2 Tim. 3:16); the whole revealed will of God in all sixty-six books of Scripture is the Christian's rule of life." The questioner uses a non-biblical term (moral law) that has been loaded with a theological meaning that was not drawn from texts of Scripture. It does not matter how ancient and venerable the term is, or how beneficial and acceptable its use has been to theologians, it is not the Word of God. The person is not asking a *biblical* question. He is asking a *theological* question. He is also defining the terms used in the question by *his own theological system and not with Scripture.* Whether it is intentional or not, this becomes a trap, with the wrong answer resulting in the appellation of the odious label 'antinomian.' All of this is the consequence of using non-biblical terminology as if it were a biblical text. Worse yet, the terminology is loaded with a theological bias that was not developed from texts of Scripture, but has evolved from its use as one of the 'good and necessary consequences' of a *particular system of theology.* The questioner accuses, tries, and convicts as heretics all those with whom he differs. The inquisitor does this totally on the basis of his own theological terms and not with Scripture. This question does not reflect an interest in whether those so questioned believe the *Bible.* Its focus is on whether they believe *the interpretation* of the Bible as expressed in the creed. John Newton described well the situation where various groups are all convinced that they and they alone, have the 'true church.'

In essentials I agree with them all, and in circumstantials I differ no more from any of them than they differ among themselves. They all confess they are fallible, yet they all decide with an air of infallibility; for they all in their turn expect me to unite with *them,* if I have any regard to the authority and honor of the Lord Jesus as Head of the Church. But the very consideration they propose restrains me from uniting with any of them. For I cannot think that I should honor the headship and kingly office of Christ by acknowledging Him as the Head *of a party* and subdivision of His people to the exclusion of the rest.

Every party uses fair sounding words of liberty; but when an explanation is made, it amounts to little more than this: that they will give me liberty to think as *they* think, and to act as *they* act; which to me, who claim the right of thinking for myself and acting according to the dictates of my own conscience, is no liberty at all. I therefore came to such conclusions as these: that I would love them all, that I would hold friendly intercourse with them all, so far as they should providentially come in my way [and, he might have added,

so far as they will allow me! A.W.P.] but that I would stand fast in
the liberty with which Christ has made me free, and call none of
them master; in fine, that if others sought to honor Him by laying
great stress on matters of doubtful disputation, my way of honoring
Him should be by endeavoring to show that His kingdom is not of
this world, nor consists in meats and drinks, in pleading for forms
and parties, but in righteousness, peace, and joy in the Holy Spirit;
and that neither circumcision is anything, nor uncircumcision, but a
new creature, and the faith which worketh *by love*.[30]

In some cases, men realize exactly what they are doing. However, they continue with their practice simply because that is the
only method they have of protecting a theological position that
they cannot textually prove with the Bible. The attitude and defense of such people is identical to that of an Arminian when he
is asked to discuss the ninth chapter of the book of Romans.
When a cherished 'system' is challenged with the Word of God
itself, some self-appointed defenders of 'God's truth' feel threatened and reach for creeds, labels, and anything else they can use
to justify their refusal to discuss the Bible itself. How else can we
explain why some people are so afraid of confronting and discussing verses of Scripture?

As mentioned earlier, when a person says, "The Ten Commandments are my rule of life," that person is actually saying,
"The tables of the covenant that established and governed the life
and worship of Israel is my rule of life today." *Both statements
mean exactly the same thing.* If we cannot assert *both* of those
statements, then we have no biblical right to voice *either one of
them.* We can no more say, "the *Ten Commandments,* as they are
given in either Exodus 20 or Deuteronomy 5, comprise the Christian's rule of life," than we can say, *"the tablets of the testimony*
that established the terms of the covenantal relationship of God
with Israel is the church's rule of life today." If we were to say,
"The Ten Commandments, as they are *individually interpreted
and applied by Christ,* are *one essential part* of the church's rule

---

[30] John Newton, quoted in A. W. Pink, *An Exposition of Hebrews,* (Swengel,
PA: Bible Truth Depot), 3:330.

of life," then we would be speaking biblically as a New Covenant believer. We could also say, "The enduring and unchanging moral principles that underlie the duties *contained* in the Ten Commandments are an important *basis* for our moral duty today." However, both of these statements are different from, "The Ten Commandments are the rule of life for a Christian today."

When we make such statements, we in no way either disparage Moses or deny that a Christian is under clear objective moral commandments as a rule for his life. Christ is a new lawgiver and his laws are more extensive than anything Moses ever imagined. The words written on the tablets of stone were the fullest revelation of moral standards ever given *up to that point in time.* However, they are *not a complete enough* standard for a child of grace who is indwelled by the Holy Spirit and lives under the New Covenant. It is unjust for anyone to call another person an 'antinomian' (which means 'against law') for teaching and insisting that the laws of Christ are *higher laws* than those given to Israel on the tables of stone. How can recognition of a fuller, more complete revelation of God's moral character be in any way construed as being anti-law? Using identical logic, I could label anyone who rejects what I have said in this book as being 'anti-Christ.' This would be an unfair and illogical charge. However, it would be no more so than labeling a person an antinomian just because he does not believe the law of Moses is not a *high enough standard* for the Christian!

It is rather surprising when we take a concordance and look up the occurrences in Scripture of the words 'law' and 'laws.' After Exodus 20, we find both words on nearly every page. However, we do not find the word 'law' (singular) used even one time in Scripture before Exodus 20. If we take Paul literally when he talks about 'until the law' and 'the law entered' (Rom. 5:13, 20) we should not expect to find the term 'the law' mentioned prior to Mount Sinai. We do find the word 'laws' (plural) used once. It is in connection with Abraham keeping God's laws (Gen. 26:5), but neither the text nor context identifies those laws except for the law of circumcision.

Our goal in this book is clearly enunciated by Paul in 1 Corinthians 9:19-21.

Though I am free and belong to no man, I make myself a slave to everyone, to win as many as possible.

To the Jews I became like a Jew, to win the Jews. To those under the law I became like one under the law (though I myself am not under the law), so as to win those under the law.

To those not having the law I became like one not having the law (though I am not free from God's law but am under Christ's law), so as to win those not having the law. (NIV)

I want to correctly represent our Lord and his glorious gospel of grace to all men. I realize some men are "under the law" in a wrong sense and others are under the wrong law. I want it clearly understood that we are not "under the law" in the sense that Israel was under the law, but we are nonetheless not lawless. We are indeed under God's true law, the law of Christ. God's true, full, and final law is given to us by our Lord Jesus Christ, whom I consider a true lawgiver who replaces Moses in exactly the same way that he replaces Aaron as our priest. I would no more think of sending a New Covenant believer back to the Old Covenant lawgiver to find God's will for the church's life and worship than I would send a believer back to Aaron or his ministry to find assurance of forgiveness of sins.

The one question I have sought to answer has nothing at all to do with whether a Christian is duty bound to obey God's clear commandments. We all agree that one of the marks of any true child of God is obedience to God's revealed will. The question is not whether we follow objective commandments or some nebulous feeling called love. Again, we agree that God's truth comes in *words*; in propositional absolutes as well as clear principles. The controversy occurs when we insist that we start and finish our ethics with the Cross and not with Mount Sinai. What are the practical implications of what I am saying for the church as a whole and the individual Christian? Is this just much ado about nothing? I believe it is a serious mistake to exalt a theological position by lowering, even if unconsciously, the standard of biblical holiness, which I believe is what Covenant Theology does.

If the Sermon on the Mount and the New Covenant Epistles do indeed teach a higher and more spiritual standard of holy living than the law of Moses, do we not effectively, in the very name of holiness, lower the actual standard of holiness under which a Christian is to live when we send him back to Moses to learn ethics and morality? Is that not exactly what Covenant Theology does? Granted they do it because they sincerely believe that Moses was the greatest lawgiver that ever lived and the law that God gave to him, Moses, was "THE full, final, eternal, unchanging moral law of God." They also are forced to insist, "Jesus Christ cannot and does not give any laws that change in any way 'the moral law' written on the tables of stone."

The bottom line is the authority of the lordship of Christ in relationship to the authority of Moses. Is Moses the final and full lawgiver and Christ merely the true interpreter and enforcer of Moses, or is Christ the new lawgiver who supersedes and replaces Moses with higher laws? It is one or the other? Are Moses and Christ really equal authorities over the church and the Christian's conscience? Was Peter, after all, correct in his desire to build one tabernacle each for Moses, Elijah, and Christ?

In reality, classical Covenant Theology produces a two-tiered system of morality and holiness. Unhappily, Moses occupies the top tier. Let me give a practical illustration to not only prove this point but also demonstrate how it works itself out in pastoral preaching and practice. Suppose a married couple comes into a pastor's study for counseling. There is no hint that they have broken God's law by being unfaithful, but the marriage is nonetheless in real trouble. Do you get the picture? Do you realize what I have just done? I have redefined the biblical commands of marriage in terms of a two-tiered ethic. I have used 'unfaithful' to mean only sexual immorality and a breach of 'God's holy law' written on stone. I have also clearly implied that whatever biblical rules of marriage the couple may have violated, those rules are not in the same category as 'God's *real* laws' written on stone.

It is obvious that one, or both, of these two people have been very unfaithful and disobedient to some things that the Word of God teaches about marriage. However, with a two-tiered ethic, you have real commandments, ten of them in fact, and you also have excellent spiritual advice found in the epistles of the New Testament Scriptures. These rules given by Paul, and others, are excellent spiritual advice and are essential to a successful marriage, but they are on a lower tier than 'THE moral Law of God.'

What will the pastor say to this couple? He will NOT go back to the tablets of stone because (1) none of those 'unchanging laws' were broken, and (2) none of the ten directly apply to the present problem, since neither party 'broke the law' by being unfaithful. The couple violated or disobeyed the theology of marriage given by Paul in his epistles but they did not 'break the law.' The pastor will go to the epistles of Paul (the lower ethical tier), and start with the truth of the Cross. He will earnestly plead, on the ground of redemption (not unchanging moral law), for the couple to begin to apply the spiritual principles that Paul lays out. He assures them that this is the only way to have a happy marriage.

In essence, the pastor is saying, "I urge you to apply these biblical principles, but what ever you do, don't break God's law and commit adultery." The Ten Commandments are foremost on the top tier; disobedience to them leads to church discipline. Paul's epistles are excellent spiritual advice, but not on a level with 'God's law'; disobedience to them will lead to more counseling sessions. My dear reader, this is not caricature or make-believe. That scene is played in many pastors' studies every day. Must we not all admit that the words of Paul do not carry the same authority over the conscience of a Christian, as do God's commandments written on tablets of stone? Must we not also admit, unless our conscience is married to a creed, that the real cause of this tragic reality is self-evident? It is the essential result of a two-tiered ethic that places the law of Moses above the words of Paul.

What am I saying? Am I suggesting that the 'advice" in the epistles of Paul is to have the same authority over the conscience of a Christian as the Ten Commandments have? No, I am saying that Paul's words should have MORE AUTHORITY! Paul's words are as equally God's words as those written on the tables of stone. If we understand progressive revelation we will see that Paul's words should and must have GREATER authority in the conscience of a New Covenant believer than anything Moses ever wrote! As long as your theology says the tables of stone are the highest standard for holiness that ever was given, it is impossible, in an experiential sense, to make the New Covenant teachings of Christ, given through his apostles by his Spirit, carry the weight of absolute law in either the life of the church or the conscience of an individual believer. It is a hollow victory that magnifies the law of Moses by minimizing the Sermon on the Mount and the epistles of Paul. You cannot posit a two-tiered ethic, with Moses on the top tier, in your theology without practicing the same thing in everyday life. Moses cannot be the lord in your principle of morality in your theology and Christ be the lord of your practice of morality in your daily life!

The greatest single tragedy that arises from misunderstanding the place and function of the Tables of the Covenant in the history of redemption is the assignment of a function to those tables that God never gave them. The Bible clearly teaches that the law must be cast out of the conscience before there can be true holiness in a believer's life. Bunyan, following Paul in Galatians 4, insists we must "cast out the law." One of the pressing questions in a discussion of law and grace is this: How could the 'holy, just and good' law of God ever produce the mob of legalist work-mongers who crucified our blessed Lord? One of the answers is simple. Why must Hagar be cast out of Abraham's house? Why cannot the son of Hagar, a bondwoman and a type of the law

(Gal. 4:21-31), be included in the inheritance with Isaac? Hagar was a wonderful handmaid, but she was never meant to be the mother of Abraham's children. The law of God is a wonderful and essential handmaid of the gospel, but was never meant by God to be the mother of holiness. All of the fruit of the law's efforts, like Ishmael, the fruit of Hagar (the law), must be cast out. The law can only produce the fruits of the flesh, which end in death.

Every attempt to produce holy living by applying Moses to the conscience is an attempt to give Moses a job God never intended him to have. It also denies the true bridegroom his full rights as the new husband.

The issue at hand is not if holiness is essential. All parties in the debate agree that of course it is! The disagreement lies in the content of the only message that can be imposed on the heart and conscience to produce the fruit that will be acceptable to God. One group says: No Moses, no holiness. I say: All Christ, holiness guaranteed. The function of the law was to convict of sin and produce death. It is most gracious when God sends his 'just, holy, good law' to kill every hope of earned forgiveness. However, when that work has been done, the law's work is finished. When we misunderstand the function of the law, we not only miss its true work, but we miss the greater glory of the New Covenant; that Jesus Christ is the fullest and final revelation of God's character.

Appendix A

Hermeneutics and the Trinity

One of the major theses in this book is the necessity of using texts of Scripture to lay the foundation blocks of any specific doctrine. We reject the notion that we can, by use of logic, establish a doctrinal point without specific textual evidence. The 'good and necessary consequences deduced' from actual texts of Scripture and the 'good and necessary consequence deduced' from the maxims of a theological system are two different things.

Our insistence on the principle of texts of Scripture as the only valid material for the foundation stones of a specific Bible doctrine has led some to accuse us of being like the Jehovah's Witnesses. One of the reasons that Jehovah's Witnesses offer for their rejection of the doctrine of the Trinity is that the word 'Trinity' is not a biblical term. There is no text of Scripture that uses that term. Within Evangelicalism, those who oppose our thesis ask, "What about the doctrine of the Trinity? Show us one verse that mentions the word Trinity. Shall we throw out the Trinity because there is no specific text that teaches that doctrine?"

This is a red herring, used by Covenant Theologians to justify theological terms like 'covenant of works with Adam' and 'the moral law' that have no textual basis in Scripture. The Westminster Confession of Faith presents these terms in this manner, "...the Lord was pleased to make a second [covenant], **commonly called**..." (Chapter 7), "...besides the law, **commonly called *moral*...**" (Chapter 19, Section 3). When the WCF uses the phrase 'commonly called,' it means, "We believe this is a biblical fact or Bible doctrine; it is essential to our system of theology, but we do not have any actual texts of Scripture to prove it." The phrase 'commonly called' means the term is used by theologians all the time.

Let me demonstrate how this comparison to the Jehovah's Witnesses is the result of fallacious reasoning. We do not reject a so-called covenant of works with Adam *only* because the word covenant is not found in Genesis 1-3, nor do we reject the idea that the Ten Commandments are the 'moral law of God' *only* because those commandments are never called that in Scripture. We reject these phrases simply because they do not represent biblical truth. Nowhere in Scripture do we find such a concept as a covenant of works with Adam whereby he could earn a kind of life that he did not already have, or the idea of 'the moral law' as covenant theologians use that term. The question is not, "Does the Bible ever use the term 'moral law?'" The question is, "Does the Bible divide the Mosaic law into three specific lists: moral, ceremonial, and civil?" Likewise the question is not, "Does the Bible use the word 'Trinity,' but rather, "Does the Word of God, with specific texts, teach the doctrine of the Trinity?" There is a great difference between the doctrine of the Trinity and the doctrine of a three-fold division of the law.

Exactly what is the doctrine of the Trinity? Let me list the individual components that comprise the doctrine of the Trinity and see if each point is derived from a specific text of Scripture.

1. **God is one God:** textual proof—*Hear, O Israel: The LORD our God is one LORD.* (Deut. 6:4)

2. **God the Father is God:** textual proof—*Labour not for the meat which perisheth, but for that meat which endureth unto everlasting life, which the Son of man shall give unto you: for him hath God the Father sealed.* (John 6:27)

3. **God the Son is God:** textual proof—*In the beginning was the Word, and the Word was with God, and the Word was God.* (John 1:1) *And the Word was made flesh, and dwelt among us, (and we beheld his glory, the glory as of the only begotten of the Father,) full of grace and truth.* (John 1:14)

4. **God the Holy Spirit is God:** textual proof—*But Peter said, Ananias, why hath Satan filled thine heart to lie to the Holy Ghost, and to keep back part of the price of the land? Whiles it remained, was it not thine own? and af-*

*ter it was sold, was it not in thine own power? why hast
thou conceived this thing in thine heart? thou hast not
lied unto men, but unto God.* (Acts 5:3,4)

5. **God is a triune God existing in three equal persons:**
    textual proof—*Go ye therefore, and teach all nations,
    baptizing them in the name of the Father, and of the Son,
    and of the Holy Ghost.* (Matt 28:19)

These texts of Scripture, when considered together, present all
the foundational elements in the doctrine of the Trinity. If God is
not both one God existing in three persons, Father, Son, and Holy
Spirit, then the Bible contradicts itself. We do not need logic or
'good and necessary consequences' to arrive at our belief in the
Trinity. Each point is proven from a text of Scripture. The only
thing we supply is a name.

We challenge anyone to take the 'commonly called' tenets in
the WCF and prove each necessary feature from Scripture. Where
does Scripture teach: Adam was under a 'probationary period'
[He may well have been, but without proof, this is mere conjec-
ture.], the length of the period, or what kind of life Adam could
'earn' by obeying this so-called covenant of works? Scripture
specifically gives death as the penalty for disobedience to the one
and only commandment recorded, but it is silent about any
'earned reward' of another kind of life.

Where in Scripture is a three-fold division of the law mentioned? Where is the concept of "THE moral law" mentioned in
even one text? To compare the doctrine of the Trinity, which can
be unquestionably established from specific texts of Scripture, to
the 'commonly called' precepts in the WCF, which have no specific texts of Scripture, is to be disingenuous. It clouds the issue
of hermeneutical integrity and discourages discussion of the actual terms the Holy Spirit used in Scripture.

Appendix B

Is there a "Moral Law of God"?

Every time I read an author who uses the term 'the moral law,' I am tempted to say, "I assume by 'moral law' that you mean the opposite of the 'immoral' law." As I understand the normal usage of that word, the opposite of moral is immoral. A moral act is the opposite of an immoral act. A moral person is the opposite of an immoral person. However, the people who employ this term in theological forms do not use the word 'moral' as the opposite of 'immoral.' They make the opposite of moral to be 'ceremonial' and 'civil.' This has created a new and unique use of the word 'moral' that is used to justify a preconceived theological position. This definition is then taken further, and without any biblical evidence, used to divide the entire Mosaic law into these three categories. People who employ this theological usage of the word 'moral' insist that the law of Moses can be divided up into three distinct lists: a 'moral law' list, a 'ceremonial law' list, and a 'civil law' list.

It is important to understand that these people use the term 'the moral law' with the same authority as if it were actually a text of Scripture. Even though they have not demonstrated with biblical evidence where this concept is taught, they treat the term as an established theological fact. They call the Ten Commandments 'the moral law,' not because it is a biblical term or even a biblical concept, but because their theological position demands it. Notice what the Westminster Confession of Faith actually states with regard to the so-called 'moral law.' In Chapter XIX, "Of The Law of God," sections I and II, the Westminster Confession states that a law was given to Adam as the basis of a "covenant of works." After man fell, this same law "continued as a perfect rule of righteousness" and as such was "given to Israel at Sinai in **ten commandments, and written in two tables**..." Section III then states, "Besides this law, **commonly called moral**..." The Ten Commandments have now officially become

"THE moral Law of God" by declaration of the framers of the Confession.

Every time I read the phrase 'commonly called' in the Confession, I want to ask, "Commonly called that **by whom?**" None of the Confession's 'commonly called' tenets are ever mentioned in the Word of God. If they were, the framers of the Confession, or their heirs, could have quoted the texts. What the Confession really means by 'commonly called' is this: "This concept is essential to our theological system. We do not have a text of Scripture to prove it, but theologians use this phrase all the time. By 'commonly called' we mean 'used all the time by theologians.'"

According to the definitions listed in Webster's Dictionary, Covenant Theology has no legitimate precedent in linguistics to make the word moral be the opposite of ceremonial and civil. The only authority for that idea is the Confession of Faith.

Here is Microsoft Word Dictionary's definition of the word 'moral' as an adjective.

1. Of or concerned with the judgment of the goodness or badness of human action and character: *moral scrutiny; a moral quandary.*

2. Teaching or exhibiting goodness or correctness of character and behavior: *a moral lesson.*

3. Conforming to standards of what is right or just in behavior; virtuous: *a moral life.*

4. Arising from conscience or the sense of right and wrong: *a moral obligation.*

5. Having psychological rather than physical or tangible effects: *a moral victory; moral support.*

6. Based on strong likelihood or firm conviction, rather than on the actual evidence: *a moral certainty.*

As a noun the word means:

1. The lesson or principle contained in or taught by a fable, a story, or an event.

2. A concisely expressed precept or general truth; a maxim.

3. Rules or habits of conduct, especially of sexual conduct, with
    reference to standards of right and wrong: *a person of loose
    morals; a decline in the public morals.*

Synonyms of the word are: *moral, ethical, virtuous, righteous.*
These adjectives mean 'in accord with principles or rules of right
or good conduct.'

1. *Moral* applies to personal character and behavior, especially
    sexual conduct, measured against prevailing standards of recti-
    tude.

2. *Ethical* stresses conformity with idealistic standards of right and
    wrong, as those applicable to the practices of lawyers and doc-
    tors.

3. V*irtuous* implies moral excellence and loftiness of character; in
    a narrower sense it refers to sexual chastity.

4. *Righteous* emphasizes moral uprightness and especially the ab-
    sence of guilt or sin; when it is applied to actions, reactions, or
    impulses, it often implies justifiable outrage.

As you can see, the word 'moral' is never used to mean something the opposite of or different from 'ceremonial.'

The word 'moral' has to do with ethical, virtuous and righteous behavior and its opposite has to do with immoral, unethical,
non-virtuous and unrighteous behavior. When 'moral' behavior is
compared to other behavior, the second behavior is always immoral, unethical or unrighteous. There is no etymological category that allows for "moral" behavior to be compared to "ceremonial" behavior. In Scripture, men are duty bound to obey every
law that God gives them. We cannot say it was Israel's 'moral
duty' to avoid adultery and their 'ceremonial duty' to be circumcised. One of those things may be, to us, moral in nature and the
other ceremonial in nature, but not to an Israelite. Both of those
duties were equal for an Israelite, and in both cases the penalty
for disobedience was death.

The concept of 'moral duty' is confusing and clearly not biblical. Nowhere in the Scriptures, either Old or New Testament, are
we told to figure out the nature of a commandment before we de-

cide whether it is our duty to obey it. We obey every law that God gives us simply because he commanded it. The key issue in this discussion concerns the appropriate means used to establish how a New Covenant Christian knows exactly which specific laws in the Bible God wants him to obey. Our response to that issue is this: "The covenant under which any person lives defines and establishes that person's rule of life." Covenant Theology proposes that the law of Moses is divided into three lists; two of those lists (the ceremonial and civil lists) are done away with, but the moral list (the Decalogue) is still in force. This becomes "the moral law" and it alone establishes our rule of life today. My view grows out of the belief that our Lord Jesus Christ is a new and greater lawgiver than Moses; Covenant Theology's view grows out of their belief that Moses was the greatest and highest lawgiver that ever lived. I insist that a new covenant based on grace, as opposed to the old covenant based on law, of necessity demands a new and higher law. Covenant Theology insists that since there is only one covenant of grace, there can only be one unchanging canon of conduct, the Ten Commandments. To make any addition or change to the words written on the tables of the covenant is to 'deny the Holy Law of God' and to risk being labeled an antinomian.

The WCF and the Philadelphia Confession of Faith, which copied the WCF, state that God gave Adam a law in the garden of Eden; this same law was written in all men after all men fell in Adam. The Confession then says, "this law, *commonly called moral* ...." (Chapter XIX, Section III). That statement is the sole source of authority used today for the division of the Mosaic law into three different lists. No writer of Scripture ever calls The Ten Commandments the moral law, nor does any writer of Scripture ever treat them as the 'eternal, unchanging, moral law of God.' It is true that the Decalogue, or tables of the covenant, received very special and unique treatment. Among other things, they were housed in a box that was so holy that no one was allowed to even touch it. However, the box was not holy because the 'moral law' was inside it, but because it housed the 'testimony,' the ta-

bles of the covenant upon which were written the Ten Commandments, or the summary of the terms of the Old Covenant. If
Covenant Theology is right in its 'eternal, unchanging, moral
law' idea then the ark would have been called the "ark of God's
moral law.'

Please do not misunderstand what I am saying. I agree with
Covenant Theology that the Bible, viewed from a New Covenant
perspective, contains laws that are clearly ethical in nature and
others laws that are ceremonial in nature. Also, there are both
civil and ceremonial laws given to Israel as a theocracy. However, nowhere does the Word of God divide the law of Moses
into these three categories or lists. Likewise, a Jew living under
the Old Covenant could not make the same distinctions that we
can make today. A Jew obeyed "the law of God" in its entirety.
He did not make sure to keep certain laws because they were on
the moral list, while not worrying too much about observance of
other laws because they were on the 'ceremonial' list. "God said"
was the Israelite's sole authority for all his behavior, whether it
concerned loving his neighbor or mixing different kind of seeds
in his garden (Lev. 19:18, 19).

The Holy Spirit has never given us a complete moral *list*, a
complete ceremonial *list,* and a complete civil *list* of laws.[31] I repeat; the idea that the Ten Commandments constitute the 'moral
law of God' is derived from the WCF, with absolutely no biblical
proof. The resultant three-fold division of law is the sole ground
for Covenant Theology's insistence that what is written on the
tablets of the covenant, or Ten Commandments, transcends all
covenant arrangements and all time.

A friend of mine came to Exodus in his daily Bible reading.
He was wrestling with the law/grace issue and New Covenant
Theology. He bought three pens of different colors and decided

---

[31] For an excellent article on the relationship of progressive revelation and idea
of "THE unchanging moral law," see chapter ten in *New Covenant Theology,*
by Tom Wells and Fred Zaspel, New Covenant Media, 5317 Wye Creek
Drive, Frederick, MD 21703-6938.

to mark the 'three different kinds of laws' in the law of Moses, and then compile them into three complete lists when he was finished. He discovered that he sometimes had to use two different colors for the same law, and even use all three colors in some verses. Sometimes, within a single passage, one colored verse would be preceded and followed by a different colored verse. He soon realized it was impossible to make any such list, simply because the Word of God never treats the law of Moses that way. The law of God given to Moses is one ball of wax and not three. Sometimes, a law that we would categorize as ceremonial in nature is considered important enough to have the death penalty attached. Examples of this are circumcision and the sabbath. There is nothing inherently sinful about picking up sticks on a particular day of the week or not being circumcised. However, when God designates those ceremonial acts as the signs of covenants, they then become the most significant duty in fulfilling the covenant stipulations.

I freely admit concurrence with the tenet that none of the laws ever change that reflect the character of God, provided that does not preclude the idea of those laws being raised to a higher level through fuller revelation. Greater revelations of God's character will, of necessity, intensify the manner of our response to that revelation. I do believe, however, that man's specific duties to God may change according to the covenant under which that man lives. This is especially true when we compare the New Covenant—upon which the Church is built—to the Old Covenant that established Israel as a nation at Sinai. The primary reason for this is that the New Covenant reveals far more of the amazing grace of God. Jesus Christ, as the exact representation of God's being (Heb. 1:3), is undeniably superior to Moses, who was faithful, but still only a servant (Heb. 3:5).

Scripture Index